THE NATURE OF
JACKSONIAN AMERICA

PROBLEMS IN AMERICAN HISTORY

EDITOR

LOREN BARITZ

State University of New York, Albany

THE FIRST PARTY SYSTEM: Federalists and Republicans
William N. Chambers

THE LEADERSHIP OF ABRAHAM LINCOLN
Don E. Fehrenbacher

THE AMERICAN CONSTITUTION
Paul Goodman

THE AMERICAN REVOLUTION
Richard J. Hooker

THE FEDERALISTS—Creators and Critics of the Union 1780-1801
Stephen G. Kurtz

AMERICA IN THE COLD WAR
Walter LaFeber

THE ORIGINS OF THE COLD WAR, 1941-1947
Walter LaFeber

AGITATION FOR FREEDOM: The Abolitionist Movement
Donald G. Mathews

THE NATURE OF JACKSONIAN AMERICA
Douglas T. Miller

AMERICAN IMPERIALISM IN 1898
Richard H. Miller

TENSIONS IN AMERICAN PURITANISM
Richard Reinitz

THE GREAT AWAKENING
Darrett B. Rutman

WORLD WAR I AT HOME
David F. Trask

THE CRITICAL YEARS,
AMERICAN FOREIGN POLICY, 1793-1825
Patrick C. T. White

THE NATURE OF
JACKSONIAN AMERICA

EDITED BY

Douglas T. Miller

John Wiley & Sons, Inc.
New York • London • Sydney • Toronto

Library of Congress Catalogue Card Number: 73-177255

ISBN 0-471-60515-8 (cloth) ;   ISBN 0-471-60516-6 (paper)

Printed in the United States of America.

10 9 8 7 6 5 4 3 2 1

For my mother
Nancy Taylor Miller

SERIES PREFACE

This series is an introduction to the most important problems in the writing and study of American history. Some of these problems have been the subject of debate and argument for a long time, although others only recently have been recognized as controversial. However, in every case, the student will find a vital topic, an understanding of which will deepen his knowledge of social change in America.

The scholars who introduce and edit the books in this series are teaching historians who have written history in the same general area as their individual books. Many of them are leading scholars in their fields, and all have done important work in the collective search for better historical understanding.

Because of the talent and the specialized knowledge of the individual editors, a rigid editorial format has not been imposed on them. For example, some of the editors believe that primary source material is necessary to their subjects. Some believe that their material should be arranged to show conflicting interpretations. Others have decided to use the selected materials as evidence for their own interpretations. The individual editors have been given the freedom to handle their books in the way that their own experience and knowledge indicate is best. The overall result is a series built up from the individual decisions of working scholars in the various fields, rather than one that conforms to a uniform editorial decision.

A common goal (rather than a shared technique) is the bridge of this series. There is always the desire to bring the reader as close to these problems as possible. One result of this objective is an emphasis on the nature and consequences of problems and events, with a de-emphasis of the more purely historiographical issues. The goal is to involve the student in the reality of crisis, the inevitability of ambiguity, and the excitement of finding a way through the historical maze.

Above all, this series is designed to show students how experienced historians read and reason. Although health is not contagious, intellectual engagement may be. If we show students something significant in a phrase or a passage that they otherwise may have missed, we will have accomplished part of our objective. When students see something that passed us by, then the process will have been made whole. This active and mutual involvement of editor and reader with a significant human problem will rescue the study of history from the smell and feel of dust.

Loren Baritz

PREFACE

For more than a century, historians have considered the second quarter of the nineteenth century to be of fundamental importance in the development of the American nation. When they have set out to define precisely what makes this period important, however, historians have not always agreed. Traditionally, the preeminence of the era was seen as resulting from its political developments. From the late nineteenth century to the years of World War II, scholars such as Frederick Jackson Turner, Charles Beard, Vernon L. Parrington, Claude Bowers, and Arthur M. Schlesinger, Jr. emphasized the victory of the Jacksonian Democrats as marking the emergence of the common man in American politics. These writers viewed the movement toward greater democracy as a powerful, popular force, uniting the majority of the people behind Andrew Jackson. They wrote in clear and simple terms about the political movement "Jacksonian Democracy" giving rise to the "Age of the Common Man."

During the past generation, however, historians have questioned nearly every aspect of this traditional interpretation. For one thing, the idea of a sudden flowering of democracy in the late 1820's and 1830's has been sharply criticized. A number of scholars have attacked the progressive dichotomy that viewed history as a recurring struggle between conservative and democratic forces. America, these authors maintain, has always been basically a middle-class, democratic society; the common man has never been submerged and, therefore, he did not dramatically reemerge as a Jacksonian Democrat in 1828. Other historians have shown that most of the democratic innovations (for instance, the extension of the suffrage) preceded the triumph of the Jacksonians and were unrelated to that movement. One recent writer rejects the entire notion of a "Jacksonian Democracy," suggesting that, if anything, the Whigs were the more innovative and liberal of the two parties. Finally, several present-day historians have argued that the egalitarian aspects of the age have been overemphasized and that the political, social, and economic equality was more rhetorical than real. In fact, not only has the dominance of the common man been challenged but also it has been claimed that the economic developments of the time helped to create sharper social stratifications.

PREFACE

These new interpretations suggest the need to reconsider the role of politics and to reevaluate the major themes of the era. This does not mean, however, that the Middle Period is less significant than was once believed. On the contrary, I would propose that it is more significant. By breaking from the previous simplistic focus on politics and democracy and by treating the era in relation to its social, economic, intellectual, and psychological realities, recent revisionist writers have discovered a highly complex age of major innovations. During the decades from the 1820s to the 1840s modern America was born, and its birth profoundly altered the subsequent course of American history.

The Jacksonian generation witnessed the transformation of the United States from a traditional, preindustrial society, which was slow to accept innovations, to a modern capitalistic nation in which people believe that society could be transformed. The revolutions in industry and transportation spawned by applied technology were the most dramatic aspects of American modernization. Equally significant, however, were the moral, psychological, ideological, and political changes in the period from the 1820s to the 1840s. A complex combination of changes made this age a modern one.

Innovations took many forms. For the first time the rate of sustained urban growth exceeded that of the population as a whole. The percentage of persons engaged in nonagricultural employment also sharply increased. From the earliest colonial settlements up until about 1815, the persons involved in commerce, industry, administration, and the professions had comprised roughly 15 percent of the population; by 1840, however, more than 36 percent of Americans were thus employed. Also during these years a notable rise in per capita income began, as industrialism became self-sustaining, and as national markets for mass-produced products developed. Rapid geographical expansion and agricultural specialization accompanied these changes.

The extent of industrial and geographical growth during the first half of the nineteenth century helped give rise to a new faith in progress. All manner of human ills, it was believed, could be overcome. A variety of would-be religious and secular utopias were conceived and established. Other persons, less visionary perhaps than the utopians, although still perfectionists, organized to rid the world of war, slavery, intemperance, and other evils. Most individuals, whether participating reformers or not, shared the faith in human betterment and believed that perfection itself could be achieved in the foreseeable future.

Yet, if the innovations of the 1820s through the 1840s gave rise to high hopes, they also created conflicts and tensions. During these years institutions and values, inherited from Europe and adapted to the American environment through the 200 years of the colonial and early national periods, were forced to adjust to rapidly altering conditions. In many cases, accustomed organizations, beliefs, and practices proved inadequate and broke down or were sharply modified. The family, for instance, traditionally a large kinship unit, of necessity became more nuclear as younger persons sought opportunities in the rising cities or on the expanding frontier. Similarly, new economic opportunities for women in industry tended to modify the traditional male and female roles. Personal relationships generally became less stable and less communal. The very belief that one's inherited economic and social status *could* be changed gave rise to the notion that it *should* be changed. Yet, there existed no secure sense of what one should achieve. The result was a confusion of values and goals. Some persons clung nostalgically to what they viewed as a receding golden age; others expressed their fears through apocalyptic images of the future. Insecurity and anxiety became hallmarks of the American character in this period and have remained so to this day.

Changes affected almost all aspects of American society in the generation after the War of 1812 and, by the end of the 1830s, it was evident that life would no longer be so simple, self-sufficient, rural, agrarian, decentralized, Anglo-Saxon, and Protestant. Both buoyant optimism and anxious uncertainties were generated as the country became more industrial, urban, centralized, and stratified, but less homogeneous and communal.

The following selections of primary sources and of recent secondary interpretations explore some of these complex changes and characteristics of the Jacksonian era. They represent, of course, only a small fragment of the available literature; however, in selecting these

PREFACE

sources an attempt has been made to deal with the major historical themes. Construed as a whole, this collection sheds a good deal of light on "the nature of Jacksonian America."*

DOUGLAS T. MILLER

East Lansing, Michigan

*For additional reading suggestions, students should consult the bibliographical essay at the end of this book.

CONTENTS

I. A TIME OF CHANGE   1

  1. Douglas T. Miller, *Everything's Changed*   3

  2. Calvin Colton, *Comparative Importance, Capabilities, and Probable Destiny of the United States; and the Relative Importance of the Mississippi Valley*   13

  3. Michael Chevalier, *Railroads in America*   17

  4. Edward Everett, *Fourth of July at Lowell*   21

II. AN AGE OF ANXIETIES   31

  5. James Kent, *No Longer to Remain Plain and Simple Republic of Farmers*   33

  6. Leo Marx, *The Machine in the Garden*   40

  7. Nathaniel Hawthorne, *The Celestial Railroad*   49

  8. Marvin Meyers, *The Jacksonian Persuasion*   57

  9. Editors of *The American Review, Inflence of the Trading Spirit Upon the Social and Moral Life of America*   70

  10. Eliza Cooke and Henry Russell, *The Old Arm Chair*   77

  11. Alexis de Tocqueville, *Causes of the Restless Spirit of the Americans in the Midst of Their Prosperity*   82

  12. Michael Chevalier, *Symptoms of Revolution*   86

III. POLITICS AND REFORM   91

  13. Richard Hofstadter, *Toward a Party System*   93

  14. Richard P. McCormick, *New Perspectives on Jacksonian Politics*   99

  15. Lee Benson, *Jacksonian Democracy—Concept or Fiction?*   113

  16. Francis J. Grund, *General Jackson Understands the People of the United States*   120

  17. John William Ward, *Andrew Jackson Symbol for an Age*   124

  18. Wendell Phillips, *Public Opinion*   129

  19. Edward Everett, *Education in the Western States*   133

  20. Ralph Waldo Emerson, *New England Reformers*   140

Bibliographical Essay   147

THE NATURE OF
JACKSONIAN AMERICA

PART ONE
A Time of Change

1 FROM *Douglass T. Miller*

History is a constant process of change—every age being both transitional and formative. Therefore, to single out a particular period as an historic watershed involves great risk of oversimplification. Nevertheless, there are eras in American history that seem to stand out as crucial turning points, decisively changing the course of the nation's development. The era of the Revolution, the Civil War, and the New Deal are such times; so, too, is the age of Jackson. On reading the opening chapters of Henry Adams' monumental history of the administrations of Jefferson and Madison, in which Adams painted a panoramic picture of society and thought in the United States around the year 1800, the student immersed in the study of Jacksonian America is struck by how remote the earlier era seems. Economic, intellectual, political, social, and psychological changes of major dimensions separate the America of the 1830s from that of the first years of the century. The following selection suggests something of the scope and significance of those changes.

In 1829, the year Andrew Jackson took office as the seventh President of the United States, John Quidor, an eccentric but

SOURCE. Douglas T. Miller, *The Birth of Modern America, 1820-1850.* copyright c 1970, by Western Publishing Company, Inc., pp. 19-21, 28-32, 34-41. Reprinted by permission of the Bobbs-Merrill Company, Inc.

brilliant artist, exhibited a painting entitled *The Return of Rip Van Winkle*. Based on Washington Irving's popular story, Quidor's painting shows a grotesque, large, bearded, old man trying to orient himself in an unfamiliar world. He appears alienated and hostile as he gazes anxiously at the strange crowd and looks for a familiar face. Around him mills the town's coarse, curious, frenzied, beardless population. Although in Irving's story Rip had fallen asleep in the period before the Revolution and awoke presumably in the 1790's, his awaking from a twenty-year sleep to discover an alien world was a better anecdote for the period in which Irving published the story, 1819; by the time Quidor illustrated Rip's return the tale had become, if anything, even more representative.[1]

Change appeared everywhere in the years following the War of 1812, and Irving and Quidor capture this in their character-izations of Rip Van Winkle. To the returning old man the transformation of society was more than that wrought by mere time. "The very character of the people seemed changed," he observed. "There was a busy, bustling, disputatious tone about it, instead of the accustomed phlegm and drowsy tranquility. . .ev-erything's changed." The town had grown larger and more populous. "There were rows of houses which he had never seen before, and those which had been familiar haunts had disap-peared. Strange names were over the doors—strange faces at the windows—everything was strange."

Many contemporaries were aware that American society was being rapidly altered in the generation after the War of 1812. "We stand this moment," stated Chancellor James Kent at New York's 1821 Constitutional Convention, "on the brink of fate, on the very edge of the precipice. . . . We are no longer to remain plain and simple republics of farmers, like New-England colonists, or the Dutch settlements on the Hudson. We are fast becoming a great nation, with great commerce, manufactures, population, wealth, luxuries, and with the vices and miseries that they engender." Three years later Daniel Webster proclaimed: "Our age is wholly of a different character, and its legislation takes another turn. Society is full of excitement. . . ." "The present," stated another

---

[1] The popularity of Irving's story increased in the Jacksonian era. In 1829 a play by John Kerr, based on Rip Van Winkle, opened in Washington and for the next generation was standard American theater fare.

American in the late 1820's, "is distinguished from every preceding age by a universal ardour of enterprise in arts and manufactures."

It would be impossible to date precisely when America changed from a tenacious, traditional society, fearful of innovation and not given to seeking riches by speculative shortcuts, to a shifting, restless, and insecure world bent on finding quicker ways to wealth than the plodding path of natural increase. But that such a shift did take place in the years between the War of 1812 and the time of Jackson is clearly evident. As Henry Cabot Lodge, who was born in 1850, noted in his *Early Memories:* "there was a wider difference between the men who fought at Waterloo and those who fought at Gettysburg or Sedan or Mukden than there was between the followers of Leonidas and the soldiers of Napoleon." To Lodge "the application of steam and electricity to transportation and communication made a greater change in human environment than had occurred since the earliest period of recorded history." In his estimate "the break between the old and the new" was completed by the 1830's. . . .

The widespread acceptance of mechanized industry and transportation might well have lagged for many years had it not been for the external circumstances that substantially cut the United States off from Europe between 1807 and 1815. Deprived of imports by the restrictive legislation of Jefferson and Madison, and blockaded by Britain following the outbreak of war in 1812, Americans were forced to manufacture their own commodities. Many wealthy merchants and shippers, suffering from the decline of trade, turned to manufacturing. The famous Lowell system was begun in 1813 when a former Boston merchant, Francis Cabot Lowell, established at Waltham the first textile factory to conduct all the operations for turning cotton into cloth by power under a single roof. By the end of the War of 1812 the factory system had a foothold, and, although manufacturing would suffer some setbacks due to heavy English importations after 1815 and the depression of 1819, America would never again be the almost exclusively agrarian society it had been in the early years of the nineteenth century.

The war years had not only been a spur to industry; they had also helped alter American attitudes, convincing many persons that true independence could come only if the nation were economically self-sufficient and had an adequate system of transportation. The spirit of nationalism that swept the country after 1815 helped sustain this sentiment. In 1816 Congress responded by passing a protective tariff and chartering the second Bank of the United States. Congress also approved a bill the following year to provide federal funds for road construction, but this was vetoed by President Madison on constitutional grounds.

Despite presidential scruples, however, internal improvements were being advanced at a rapid pace. The early success of the Lancaster turnpike in the 1790's had given rise to a boom in road building, particularly in New England and the Middle States. Construction of the federally financed National Road from Baltimore began in 1811 and by 1818 had been completed across the mountains to Wheeling on the Ohio River, making easier the settlement and development of the West. In 1817 the New York Legislature, following the advice of Governor DeWitt Clinton, authorized construction of a canal to connect the Hudson to the Great Lakes. Completed in October, 1825, the Erie Canal ran over 350 miles from Albany to Buffalo and quickly proved profitable because it created both an easy route for western emigration and a means of transporting goods cheaply and efficiently. Its success started a canal-building craze throughout the nation.

Enthusiastic support for rapid transportation became widespread. By the mid-1820's Mathew Carey, the Philadelphia publisher, economist, and social reformer, had little difficulty in getting hundreds of persons to join a Society for the Promotion of Internal Improvements with an initiation fee of $100 "to finance the dissemination of accurate information on canals, roads, bridges, railways, and steam engines." As a reporter for the *United States Gazette,* February 23, 1825, wrote: "One hundred dollars, the highest initiary fee that we recollect in our country, are demanded as the price of the privilege of serving their country in its ranks, with the certainty, that this bread cast upon the waters, can return but after many days, and *that only* in the consciousness of having been useful of other."

The early revolutions in industry and transportation had a marked effect on the American population, and did a great deal to eliminate the idleness that Henry Adams had described as characteristic at the turn of the century. George White, a staunch advocate of manufacturing and an early biographer of Samuel Slater, commented on just this change. "In districts far from markets," he wrote, men "are too apt, for want of due encouragement to industrious habits, to throw away their time in worse than useless idleness and dissipation. Whoever has experienced the difficulties attendant on almost all efforts for the moral advancement of a poor and scattered population, without this encouragement, and compares them with the facilities afforded by thriving towns and villages, inhabited and surrounded by an industrious and happy people, will see at once that whatever tends to improve the physical condition of man, must, as it renders him more comfortable, conduce, in no small degree, to the improvement of his morals. . . . "

By the time of Jackson's presidency an idle American was a rarity. Foreign travelers and native writers alike attest to the fact that haste had become a national characteristic. Returning from Europe in 1836, the sculptor Horatio Greenough saw speed as the key to American character. "Rail Roads alone seem to be *understood,*" he observed. "Go ahead! is the order of the day. The whole continent presents a scene of *scrabbling* and roars with greedy hurry." "Life consists in motion," testified Francis Grund, an Austrian who had settled in America in the late 1820's. "The United States present certainly the most animated picture of universal bustle and activity of any country in the world. Such a thing as rest or quiescence does not even enter the mind of an American. . . . This state of incessant excitement gives to the American an air of busy inquietude. . . which, in fact, constitutes their principle happiness."

Grund went on to note that "the position of a man of leisure in the United States is far from being enviable; for. . . he is not only left without companions to enjoy his luxuriant ease, but, what is worse, he forfeits the respect of his fellow citizens, who, by precept and example are determined to discountenance idleness." Even the little leisure that was allowed seemed to be taken up with nervous activity; American rocking, whittling, and chewing continually amazed foreign visitors.

Another seeming change in American values was the new openness with which persons came to accept technological innovations. While in the United States in the 1820's, Frederick List, the German economist, observed that "everything new is quickly introduced here, and all the latest inventions. There is no clinging to old ways, the moment an American hears the work 'invention' he pricks up his ears." "The inventors of machinery," stated the New York author James Kirke Paulding in the late 1820's, "have caused a greater revolution in the habits, opinions, and morals of mankind, than all the efforts of legislation. Machinery and steam engines have had more influence on the Christian world than

Locke's metaphysics, Napoleon's code, or Jeremy Bentham's codification." Machinery, in the words of Salmon P. Chase in 1832, has "freed the inherent energy of moral ideas, removed obstructions out of the way of their action, and has brought them into contact with the objects on which they are to act." That same year a writer for the *North American Review* declared: "What we claim for machinery is, that it is in modern times by far the most efficient physical cause of human improvement; that it does for civilization what conquest and human labor formerly did, and accomplishes incalculably more than they accomplished." Five years later, Edward Everett, then governor of Massachusetts, exclaimed; "The mechanician, not the magician, is now the master of life." "Are not our inventors," asked another enthusiast, "absolutely ushering in the very dawn of the millennium?". . .

As Americans became more innovative and less idle, they developed a new sense of progress. The idea of progress, of course, was not unique to the 1820's and 1830's. Many Americans of the eighteenth century believed strongly in the possibilities of progress. This was a basic tenet of Enlightenment thought, and for many persons the success of the American Revolution was vivid proof of mankind's advance. Yet for most eighteenth-century Americans, whether they viewed progress in material terms or in a more idealistic sense, the amelioration of mankind was felt to be a slow process. Furthermore, numerous doubts remained concerning the nature of man and the improvability of society. The debates at the Constitutional Convention in 1787, where even the most liberal delegates expressed certain reservations about man's innate goodness, make this quite clear.

By the late 1820's, however, doubts about progress has all but disappeared, and not only was human betterment believed possible, it was also expected to be rapid. As the historian John Thomas has pointed out, this was part of a broader change from the rational outlook of the Enlightenment to the emotional attitude associated with Romanticism. "A romantic religious faith," Thomas writes, "had changed an Enlightenment doctrine of progress into a dynamic principle of reform." The concept of progress had come to mean romantic perfectionism which demanded immediate improvement. This was reflected in such seemingly diverse Jacksonian phenomena as the President's attack on the Bank, Garrison's advocacy of immediate abolition of slavery, William Miller's prediction of an imminent millennium, and the ordinary citizen's rising material aspirations.

Another historian, Stow Persons, has described this change from the late eighteenth century to the 1820's in terms of theories of history. Persons contends that most American thinkers of the Revolutionary period, including John Adams and Thomas Jefferson, held a cyclical view of history. Nations were thought to have natural life cycles analogous to living organisms. America after the Revolution, it was believed, was in a state of youth which made it morally superior to Europe. Safeguards were needed to bolster the new nation's youthful virtue, however, since, as Jefferson warned in 1781, "the spirit of the times may alter, will alter. Our rulers will become corrupt, our people careless. A single zealot may commence persecuter, and better men be his victims." America's enviable position was precarious and ultimately likely to dissipate. Its continuance depended on preserving moral virtues, which for Jefferson meant maintaining an agrarian way of life.

Gradually, however, in the early nineteenth century the cyclical theory came to seem less relevant to Americans; it became more common to see this nation's history in terms of progress alone. Suggestive of this changing view were Jefferson's thoughts on history in his latter years. "Science," he wrote to John Adams, October 28, 1813, "had liberated the ideas of those who read and reflect, and the American example had kindled feelings of right in the people. An insurrection has consequently begun, of science, talents and courage against rank and birth, which have fallen into contempt. . . .Science is progressive, and talents and enterprise on the alert." Even the more conservative Adams in old age also abandoned the cyclical theory in favor of progressive belief. Writing to Jefferson in 1821 he stated: "You and I hope for splendid improvements in human society, and vast amelioration in the condition of mankind. Our faith may be supported by more rational arguments than any former. I own that I am very sanguine in the belief of them as I hope and believe you are. . . ." The changing views of Jefferson and Adams, remarkable in their own right for men of that age, mirrored those of society generally, and by the 1820's, as Persons concludes, the idea of progress had become "the fighting faith of men with a mission to perform, whether to feed the hungry, convert the heathen, or accumulate one's pile."

The strong faith in progress tended to make Americans always slightly dissatisfied with the present but expectant of a better future. "It is peculiarly the happy privilege of Americans," stated William James, a wealthy New York contractor and grandfather of the philosopher and the novelist, "to enjoy the blessings of hope and expectation." The expectations most commonly shared by Jacksonian Americans were unquestionably economic. "'*Go ahead*' is the real motto of the country," proclaimed a foreign traveler, "and every man does push on, to gain in advance of his neighbour." Alexis de Tocqueville was struck by the fact that "it is not only a portion of the people which is busied with the amelioration of its social condition, but the whole community is engaged in the task." "How widely spread," noted William Ellery Channing, "is the passion for acquisition, not for simple subsistence, but for wealth! What a rush into all departments of trade."

Given the passion for wealth that dominated most Americans, it is not surprising to find that this era gave rise to the cult of the "self-made man." [2] Journalists, clergymen, lawyers, and others reiterated that anything was possible. Jackson himself, an orphan and clearly self-made, was a fitting symbol for the age. Examples of persons inspired to new aspirations by the rags-to-riches philosophy are many. Thomas Mellon, the founder of that family's fortune, recalled that as a young man of fourteen in 1828 he had been motivated by the dream of economic betterment through reading the classic American success story Franklin's *Autobiography.* "I had not before imagined," Mellon wrote, "any other course of life superior to farming, but the reading of Franklin's life led me to question this view. For so poor and friendless a boy to be able to become a merchant or a professional man had before seemed an impossibility; but here was Franklin poorer than myself, who by industry, thrift and frugality had become learned and wise, and elevated to wealth and fame." Mellon soon left the family farm at Poverty Point and moved to nearby Pittsburgh where he quickly advanced as a lawyer, money lender, and finally banker.

That Mellon's quest for fortune led him from farm to city was not unusual for the age. Although agriculture remained the leading economic pursuit through the pre-Civil War period, ambitious Americans like Mellon were turning to more rapidly rewarding occupations in such fields as commerce and manufacturing. "My disposition," wrote a young man in 1818, "would not allow me to work on a farm. . . .I thought that I should be one of

---

[2] The term "self-made man" was first coined, according to the historian of this subject, Irvin Wyllie, by Henry Clay in 1832.

the happiest fellows in the world if I could only be rich, and I thought as others had begun with nothin and become men of fortune that I might. . . ."

One result of the rising economic expectations and consequent attractiveness of nonagrarian pursuits was the great urban growth of the era. Up to about 1820 the expansion of cities had been slow at best. In fact America had a larger percentage of urban dwellers in relation to the total population in 1700 (ca. ten per cent) than a century later when about six per cent of the people could be classified as urban. The rate of urbanization picked up slightly between 1800 and 1810, reaching 7.3 per cent by the latter date. But in the next decade, westward expansion and lack of immigration actually caused the city population to increase at a slightly slower rate than the population generally and by 1820 only 7.2 per cent of the people lived in cities. The decade of the twenties, however, reversed this trend and began the rapid urbanization of the nation which would be so significant in differentiating modern America from its rural past. By 1830 approximately ten per cent of Americans were city dwellers. By 1860 this percentage had doubled in the most rapid period of urban growth in the nation's history. Between 1820 and 1840 Philadelphia and its immediate suburbs had grown from about 100,000 to well over 200,000; Pittsburgh during these same decades went from slightly over 7,000 to more than 21,000; New York, America's major metropolis, swelled from 123,000 to over 312,000 in these twenty years; while cities such as Lowell and Chicago which had not existed prior to 1820 were fast becoming major centers. In short, the rise of the modern city has been a fairly recent phenomenon beginning about the age of Jackson.

Rapid urbanization, improved transportation, industrialization, new technological innovations, westward expansion, increased mobility, rising aspirations, and greater wealth were rapidly altering American society during the 1820's and 1830's. By the time Jackson assumed the presidency, America appeared young, buoyant, and expanding. Optimism was widespread. The nation presents a "scene of unmingled prosperity and happiness," declared a Jacksonian Fourth of July orator. The ordinary citizen, he continued, has "his aspirations lifted up to the most exalted objects. . . ."

So abundant and promising did the future seem that most American economists, whether free-traders or protectionists, rejected the gloomy theories of Thomas Malthus. Hezekiah Niles, the indefatigable publisher of Niles' Weekly Register, held that in the United States the population, far from being excessive and a cause of poverty, constituted "The strength and wealth of our country. . . ." Henry Carey, the son of Mathew Carey and one of this country's most original economists, wrote in 1835: "Mr. Malthus tells us, that wherever food is abundant, population increases rapidly; but it might be correctly said, that where population increases rapidly, food is abundant, and we have full evidence that with increased population, the dangers of famine are greatly decreased, where man is not too much trammeled."

Yet American optimism, real though it was, was not the only sentiment prevalent. This was also a time of tensions and insecurities. The speed of social and economic change in these years could not help but generate uncertainties. Prior to 1815, America had been a fairly stable society for nearly two centuries; except for the Revolution, changes had occurred gradually and within accustomed institutional frameworks. After that date, however, new technology, new forms of economic organization, and newly enriched persons presented a challenge to the old certitudes. The traditional moral values were not always consonant with the emerging practices of American capitalism. Restlessness and inner tensions resulted. The look of alienation on Rip Van Winkle's face as painted by John Quidor was indeed representative of a growing attitude which many Americans shared in confronting the changing social scene. . . .

2 FROM   *Calvin Coltar*
Comparative Importance, Capabilities, and
Probable Destiny of the United States;
and the Relative Importance of the Mississippi Valley

Calvin Colton was a booster of America. A Yale graduate, Colton began his career as a minister, but he turned increasingly to writing and politics in the 1830s. He became a highly successful Whig editor and essayist, and the official biographer of Henry Clay.

In this selection, written for the elucidation of prospective European emigrants to America, Colton captures the optimistic attitude most Americans shared concerning the nation's future. Notice particularly the importance placed on the westward movement away from Europe into the Mississippi Valley, and on the expressed belief that "the providence of God" directed America's happy destiny.

The importance of a nation is *physical* and *moral* . Its physical importance consists *generally* in the extent and resources of its soil, and its commercial advantages. The *moral* power of a nation is estimated by the amount and character of the population, and by the nature of its institutions. Population is also a component element of the physical power of a community.

The number of square miles in all Europe is about 3,400,000— Russia claiming nearly half of this. The territorial jurisdiction of the United States is equal to *three-fourths* of all Europe. And the resources of its soil, and its commercial advantages, all things considered, cannot be considered inferior to Europe. Each of the twenty-four United States, on an average, is nearly as large as the whole of England *proper.* And the Territory, not yet organized into States, is vastly larger than that which is.

The present actual population of the United States will only compare with some of the individual States of Europe. It is less

SOURCE. Calvin Colton, *Manual for Emigrants to America* (London, F. Westley and A.H. Davis, 1832), pp. 120-129.

than half of the population of France, and about two-thirds of the population of Great Britain and Ireland. But the past and prospective increase of population in the United States is prodigious. It doubles at least once in twenty-five years. By this rule, the present population being assumed as 13,000,000, in 1857 it will be 26,000,000; in 1882 it will be 52,000,000; in 1907 it will be 104,000,000; and, in 1932, or in one hundred years from this time, it will be 208,000,000! In one hundred and fifty years, it will be 832,000,000—equal to the present population of the globe! Assuming the permanency of the Government of the United States—in the maintenance of the integrity of the Union, on the ground of the Federal Compact, with an ordinary degree of prosperity, however amazing these results may seem, a large moiety of them may be set down as *probable* against all contingencies. Bating the effects of foreign war, and of internal and violent disruptions, a growth of this kind would seem to be a physical certainty; the former of which is hardly to be expected, so as to afford a serious check to such advancement, inasmuch as there is no rival power on the Continent of America, and the Republic is too remote to be reduced by invasion from another Continent. And as to internal disruption, it is *possible,* but not probable to occur, with such calamity in its train, as to disappoint a destiny sufficiently bright and cheering to satisfy any reasonable ambition. The destiny of the United States is reasonably rescued from the ordinary calculations of historical *data,* inasmuch as the providence of God never yet set up a nation of a like character, in like circumstances. It is thrown completely without the pale of ordinary political prognostication. There are no premises in the history of nations bearing resemblances sufficient to found a prediction of overthrow in the present instance, within the scope of a statesman's ken—unless it be, that that which *both* not been, *cannot* be—which is disproved in the threshold, that that which hath not been, already *is;*—viz. a nation without a *type* in character and circumstance. Those who deal so generously in their predictions of a disastrous issue to the Republic of the United States, only show their ignorance of the nature of its Government, and of the moral character of the community. Every severe test, as yet, has only contributed to cement and consolidate the Union. And whatever doubt there may have been of the perpetuity of the Government, in all its purity and energy, there is less doubt now than ever. The world at a distance, witnessing the occasional violent irruptions of party feeling in the United States from a particular quarter, and

on some local, or even general question, and listening to the
stormy rancour of some newspaper declaimers, and perhaps of
parliamentary debates, might imagine that the Republic was in
jeopardy, and the Union about to be dissolved; whereas, all these
agitations, instead of disjointing the general fabric of the community, only settle it down more firmly on its own proper
foundations. . . .

And as to the *capabilities* of the United States, both physical and
moral, such as they are now, in fact, and such as they are in
prospect—there is no arithmetic of man that can estimate them.

And the great bulk of these capabilities, prospectively, lie in the Valley
of the Mississippi. It is there they are to be developed and
demonstrated. In twenty years, the bulk of the population will be
there. In half a century, the *nation* will be there; so that, every
thing found on the Atlantic declivity, east of the Alleghanies,
although it was originally *itself* the nation, and although it shall
still be growing in the meantime, will not withstanding be left only
a skirt. There, in the Mississippi Valley, beyond a question, and in
a very brief time, will be cities and towns to rival any in the world
in population, in commercial enterprise, in the productions of art,
in the refinements of cultivated life and manners—and, I fear, in
luxury. There, in that vast region, compared with which, in
geographical extent, the whole of Europe on this side of Russia, is
no more than equal,—will be found, within half a century, a
teeming, active, industrious population, themselves a *world!*—still
increasing with unexampled rapidity, and crowding still more
densely the place, which shall have become too strait for them—
and sending out their swarms towards the shores of the Pacific.
Then, instead of three hundred steam-boats, more or less, now in
active employment, will be *thousands,* shooting up and down the
channels of its rivers—and where the natural channels fail, canals
and railways will supply their place, to connect every smaller and
more remote district with every other, and to bring the market of
the world near to every point.

There is nothing visionary, or improbable in all this. It is even
now as certain, as that the world shall endure, and the family of
man multiply upon the face of it. Nor need we trouble ourselves at
present to bring in the benefit of Mr. Malthus's theory to save this
Valley from being deluged with a population beyond its physical
resources to sustain. Much more would it be a premature anxiety
and a rare waste of benevolence, to contrive to bring in war, and

famine, and pestilence, and earthquake, to assist the high Providence above in maintaining his own offspring, and in keeping their increase within just limits, as to save them from starvation, and leave them place to set a foot upon. We hope mankind will yet become too good to kill one another—too temperate and virtuous to fall victims of vice—and so observant of the precepts of Heaven, as not to provoke Heaven's exterminating judgments;—and that that period is not far distant. And as to the earth's being *overrun*, He who made and peopled it will take care of that; and, if necessary, will, peradventure, anticipate such a catastrophe by some change in the economy of his providence—such, for example, as the conflagration of the world, and the introduction of the human family, when they shall have become worthy, to a higher and nobler state of existence. It is to be hoped, that all this reasoning, predicated on the *vices* of mankind, in its prophecies of the future, will yet find reason to shift its ground, and assume for its premises the *virtues* of a better era of the world. And, for one, I have no objection that America should present the first example— the first array of facts in the economy of human society, to dissolve this dark and gloomy spell of evil boding to man. It is unnecessary to my present purpose, however, that I should prove all this—It is enough to have shown that America presents an open field for a mighty and an incalculable population;—that it is evidently destined to such importance—that the providence of God has set up a state of society and a Government there of hopeful and high promise;—that from the peculiarity of its institutions, and in consideration of its remoteness from rival interests, it is not likely soon to be shaken, or disturbed in its foundations;—and, above all,—if, from the gleamings and faith of *divine* prophecy, it may be hoped that the world is on the eve of a better state,—that the American Government and institutions shall *never* be overthrown, but will be improved in their forms, and ultimately arrive at the *perfection* of the constitution of human society. That those who have been used only to a Government of physical force, should reason differently, is not strange.

3 FROM *Michael Chevalier*
Railroads in America

Central to the restless optimism of Jacksonian Americans was a revolution in transportation. The years after 1815 saw the widespread adoption of steamboats and the construction of numerous turnpikes and canals, capped by the completion of the 360-mile Erie Canal in 1825. Even more dramatic was the adoption of railroads. When Jackson was first elected to the presidency in 1828, only a few miles of track had been laid. By the end of the 1830s, however, there were nearly 3000 miles of road; by 1860 railroad mileage exceeded 30,000.

One of the keenest early witnesses of the impact of rapid transportation on te Americhan society was the Frenchman, Michael Chevalier, who spent two years in the United States (1833 to 1835) on a mission for his government to study technological improvements, particularly in transportation. As Chevalier observed, America's "most suitable emblem would be a locomotive engine or a steamboat."

Some days ago I happened to be in the little city of Petersburg, which stands at the falls of the Appomattox and near which there is an excellent railroad. A merchant of the city took me to a manufactory of tobacco in which some peculiar processes were employed. In these works was manufactured that sort of tobacco which most Americans chew and will chew for some time to come in spite of the severe, but in this matter just, censures of English travelers, unless the fashion of vetoes should spread in the United States and the women should set theirs on the use of tobacco with as unyielding a resolution as the President has shown toward the Bank. After having wandered about the workshops amid the poor little slaves by whom they are filled, I was stopping to look at some of these blacks, who appeared to me almost white and who had

SOURCE. Michael Chevalier, *Society, Manners and Politics in the United States: Being a Series of Letters on North America* (Boston, Weeks, Jordan and Company, 1839), pp. 83-87.

not more than one eighth of African blood in their veins, when my companion said to me, "As you are interested in railroads, you must see the one belonging to the works." Accordingly we went to the room where the tobacco is packed in kegs and subjected to a powerful pressure. The apparatus for pressing is a very peculiar contrivance—I will not now stop to describe it—the most important part of which is a movable railroad, suspended from the ceiling. Thus the Americans have railroads in the water, in the bowels of the earth, and in the air. The benefits of the invention are so palpable to their practical good sense that they endeavor to make an application of it everywhere and to everything, rightly or wrongly. When they cannot construct a real, profitable railroad across the country from river to river, from city to city, or from State to State, they get one up, at least as a plaything or until they can accomplish something better, under the form of a machine.

The distance from Boston to New Orleans is sixteen hundred miles, or twice the distance from Havre to Marseilles. It is highly probable that within a few years this immense line will be covered by a series of railroads stretching from bay to bay, from river to river, and offering to the ever-impatient Americans the service of their rapid cars at the points where the steamboats leave their passengers. This is not a castle in the air, like so many of those grand schemes which are projected amid the fogs of the Seine, the Loire, and the Garonne. It is a fact already half realized. The railroad from Boston to Providence is in active progress; the work goes on *a lamericaine,* that is to say, rapidly. From New York to Philadelphia, there will soon be not only one open to travel, but two in competition with each other, the one on the right, the other on the left bank of the Delaware; the passage between the two cities will be made in seven hours, five hours on the railroad, and two in the steamboat on the beautiful Hudson and the magnificent Bay of New York, which the Americans who are not afflicted with modesty compare with the Bay of Naples. From Philadelphia, travelers go to Baltimore by the Delaware and Chesapeake, and by the Newcastle and Frenchtown railroad, in eight hours; from Baltimore to Washington, a railroad has been resolved upon, a company chartered, the shares taken, and the work begun, all within the space of a few months. Between Washington and Blakely, in North Carolina, 60 miles of railroad are completed, from Blakely northward. A company has just been chartered to complete the remaining distance, that is, from Richmond to the Potomac, 70 miles, and the Potomac bears you to the Federal city,

passing on the way Mount Vernon, a delightful spot, the pat-
rimony of George Washington where he passed his honored old age
and where his body now reposes in a modest tomb. Between
Washington and Blakely, those who prefer the steamboats may
take another route; by descending the Chesapeake to Norfolk, they
will find another railroad, 70 miles in length, of which two thirds
are now finished, and which carries them to Blakely, and even
beyond. Blakely is a new town which you will not find on any
map, born of yesterday; it is the eldest, and as yet the only
daughter of the Petersburg railroad. From Blakely to Charleston,
South Carolina, the distance is great, but the Americans are
enterprising and there is no region in the world in which railroads
can be constructed so easily and so cheaply; the surface has been
graded by nature and the vast forest which cover it will furnish
the wood of which the railroad will be made; for here most of
these works have a wooden superstructure. From Charleston, a
railroad 137 miles in length, as yet the longest in the world,
extends to Augusta, whence to Montgomery, Alabama, there is a
long interval to be supplied. From Montgomery, steamboats
descend the River Alabama to Mobile, and those who do not wish
to pay their respects to the Gulf of Mexico on their way to New
Orleans will soon find a railroad which will spare them the
necessity of offering this act of homage to the memory of the great
Cortez.

Within ten years this whole line will be completed and traversed
by locomotive engines, provided the present crisis terminates
promptly and happily, as I hope it will. Ten years is a long time in
these days and a plan whose execution requires ten years seems
like a romance or a dream. But in respect to railroads, the
Americans already have something to show. Pennsylvania, which
by the last census, in 1830, contained only 1,348,000 inhabitants,
has 325 miles of railroads actually completed or which will be so
within the year, without reckoning 76 miles which the capitalists
of Philadelphia have constructed in the little States of New Jersey
and Delaware. The total length of all the railroads in France is 95
miles, that is, a little more than what the citizens of Philadelphia,
in their liberality, have given to their poor neighbors. In the State
of New York, whose population is the most adventurous and the
most successful in their speculations, there are at present only four
or five short railroads, but if the sixth part of those which are
projected and authorized by the legislature are executed, New
York will not be behind Pennsylvania in this respect. The

merchants of Baltimore, which at the time of the Declaration of Independence contained 6,000 inhabitants, and which now numbers 100,000, have taken it into their heads to make a railroad between their city and the Ohio, a distance of above 300 miles. They have begun it with great spirit and have now finished about one third of the whole road. In almost every section east of the Ohio and the Mississippi there are railroads projected, in progress, or completed, and on most of them locomotive steam engines are employed. There are some in the Alleghenies, whose inclined planes are really terrific because of their angle of climb; these were originally designed only for the transportation of goods, but passenger cars have been set up on them at the risk of breaking the necks of travelers. There are here works well constructed and ill constructed; there are some that have cost dear (from $40,000 to $50,000 a mile), and others that have cost little (from $10,000 to $15,000 a mile). New Orleans has one, a very modest one to be sure, only five miles long, but it will soon have others and, after all, it is ahead of old Orleans, for the latter has yet to wait till its capitalists, seized with some violent fit of patriotism, shall be ready to make the sacrifice of devoting some ten or twelve per cent of their capital to the construction of a railroad thence to Paris. Virginia, whose population is nearly the same as that of the Department of the North in France, and which is inferior in wealth, already has 75 miles of railroad fully completed and 110 in progress, exclusive of those begun this year. The Department of the North, where it would be quite as easy to construct them and where they would be more productive, has not a foot completed or in progress and hardly a foot projected. Observe, moreover, that I here speak of railroads alone, the rage for which is quite new in America, while that for canals is of very old date (for in this country fifteen years is an age) and has achieved wonders. There are States which contain 500, 800, or 1,000 miles of canals. We in France are of all people the boldest in theory and speculation and we have made the world tremble by our political experiments; but during the last twenty years we have shown ourselves the most timid of nations in respect to physical improvements.

4 FROM Edward Everett
Fourth of July at Lowell

Indicative of the growing importance of industrialism was the emergence of Lowell, Massachusetts. Established by a group of wealthy Boston investors in 1823 as a center for the manufacture of cotton cloth, Lowell flourished and quickly became the showplace of American industry. By the late 1820s, Lowell's factories with their thousands of New England farm-girl laborers had become an accustomed stop on the itineraries of traveling foreign and native dignitaries. The lavish praise heaped on Lowell's paternalistic enterprise by distinguished visitors helped to create a progressive industrial image acceptable to agrarian America.

In the 1830 Fourth of July oration that follows, Edward Everett, a noted lecturer, scholar, and Whig politician, praises Lowell "as a specimen of other similar seats of American art and industry." Using Lowell as a symbol of progress, Everett assured his audience that such "astonishing growth" could only "be considered as a peculiar triumph of our political independence."

Fellow-citizens of Lowell,. . . your town itself, in its very existence, affords signal authority for doing things at short notice. If, on the fourth of July, 1820,—ten years ago only,—a painter had come to the confluence of the Merrimack and Concord Rivers, and sketched upon his canvas the panorama of such a city as this, and pronounced that, in ten years, such a settlement would be found on this spot, it would have been thought a very extravagant suggestion. If he had said that, in the course of forty or fifty years, such a population would be gathered here, with all these manufacturing establishments, private dwellings, warehouses, schools, and churches, he would have been thought to indulge a bold, but pleasing, vision, not, perhaps, beyond the range of probability. The Roman history contains a legend of the Seven Sleepers of

SOURCE. Edward Everett, *Orations and Speeches on Various Occasions* (4 vols., 9th edition, Boston, Little, Brown, and Company, 1878-1879), II, pp. 47-55.

Ephesus, who, having prolonged their slumbers to the unusual extent of two hundred and seventy years, were a good deal bewildered, when they awoke, to find a new emperor on the throne, strange characters on the coin, and other very considerable innovations. A person who should have gone to sleep in one of the two farm-houses which, ten years ago stood on the site of Lowell, would have found greater changes on waking.

Finally, my friends, without wishing to run down the idea, I may remark, that our whole country has taken her present position in the family of nations on very short notice. Our history seems a great political romance. In the annals of most other states, ancient and modern, there is a tardiness of growth, which, if our own progress be assumed as the standard of comparison, we hardly know how to explain. Greece had been settled a thousand years before she took any great part on the theatre of the world. Rome, at the end of five centuries from the foundation of the city, was not so powerful as the state of Massachusetts. . . .

What do we witness in this country? Compare our present condition with that of this then barbarous wilderness two centuries ago. With what rapidity the civilization of Europe has been caught up, naturalized, and, in many points of material growth and useful art, carried beyond the foreign standard! Consider our rapid progress even in the last generation, not merely in appropriating the arts of the old world, but in others of our own invention or great improvement. Take the case of steam navigation as a striking example. It has been known, for a century or more, that the vapor of boiling water is the most powerful mechanical agent at our command. The steam engine was brought near to perfection, by Bolton and Watt, sixty years ago; and it is not much less than that time since attempts began to be made to solve the problem of steam navigation. Twenty years ago, there were steamers regularly plying on the North River and Staten Island Sound; but so lately as eleven years ago, I think, there was no communication by steam between Liverpool and Dublin, or between Dover and Calais; nor did the use of steamers spread extensively in any direction in Europe till they had covered the American waters.

Take another example, in the agricultural staple so closely connected with the industry of Lowell. The southern parts of Europe, Egypt, and many other portions of Africa, and a broad zone in Asia, possess a soil and climate favorable to the growth of cotton. It is, in fact, an indigenous product of Asia, Africa, or

both. It has been cultivated in those countries from time immemorial: the oldest European historians speak of its use. It is,
also, an indigenous product throughout a broad belt on the
American continent; and was cultivated by the aborigines before
the discovery of Columbus. Although it was the leading principle
of the colonial system to encourage the cultivation in the colonies
of all those articles which would be useful to the manufactures of
the mother country, not a bale of cotton is known to have been
exported from the United States to Great Britain before the
revolution. Immediately after the close of the revolutionary war,
attention began to be turned to this subject in several parts of the
Southern States. The culture of cotton rapidly increased; and,
since the invention of the cotton gin, has become, next to the
cereal grains, the most important agricultural product. It is
supposed, that, for the present year, the cotton crop of the United
States will amount to one million of bales—five times, I presume,
the amount raised for exportation in all the rest of the world.

Take another example, in commerce and navigation, and one
peculiarly illustrative of the effect, on the industry of the country,
of the political independence established on the day which we
commemorate. The principles of the colonial system confined our
trade and navigation to the intercourse of the mother country.
The individuals are living, or recently deceased, who made the
first voyages from this country to the Baltic, to the Mediterranean,
or around either of the great capes of the world. Before the
declaration of independence, the hardihood and skill of our
mariners had attracted the admiration of Europe. Burke has
commemorated them in a burst of eloquence which will be
rehearsed as long as the English language is spoken. But though he
exclaims, "No sea but what is vexed by their fisheries, no climate
that is not witness to their toils," the commerce and navigation of
the colonies are scarce worthy of mention, in comparison with
those of the United States. All that Burke admired and eulogized is
inconsiderable, when contrasted with what has been achieved, in
this respect, since the declaration of independence.

Nor is the progress less remarkable which has been made since
that event in the interior of the continent. The settlement of our
western country is a marvel in human affairs. This great enterprise, as we know, languished under the colonial government. For
this there were many reasons. The possessions of France, with
powerful native tribes in her alliance, stretched along the frontier,
from the Gulf of the St. Lawrence to that of Mexico. A certain

density of population along the coast was, of necessity, a condition precedent to the settlement of the region west of the Alleghanies; and then this subject attracted the attention of the mother country, the extension of the plantations beyond the Ohio was forbidden, for reasons of state. With the declaration of independence,—notwithstanding the burdens and discouragements of the war of the revolution, and the hostility of the formidable tribes of savages who sided with Great Britain,— the hardy column of emigrants, with Daniel Boone at their head, forced its way over the mountains, and conquered and settled Tennessee and Kentucky. As soon as the pacification of the north-western tribes and the surrender of the British posts made it practicable, the enterprising youth of New England, and, among the foremost, those of Essex and Middlesex, in this state, took up the line of march to Ohio; and now the three states which I have named, which, before the revolution, did not contain a regular white settlement, are inhabited by a population equal to that of the thirteen colonies at the beginning of the revolutionary war.

This astonishing growth has evidently not only been subsequent to the declaration of independence, but consequent upon its establishment, as effect upon cause; and this both by a removal of specific obstacles to our progress, which were imposed by the colonial system, and by the general operation of the new political order of things on the mind and character of the country. The reason why England has long excelled every other country in Europe, in the extent of her available resources, and in the cultivation of most of the practical arts, is to be found in those principles of constitutional representative government, in that parliamentary freedom and popular energy which cannot exist under any form of despotism. The still more complete establishment of similar principles here, I take to be the chief cause of a still more accelerated march of improvement. It is usual to consider human labor as the measure of value. That which can be got by any one without labor, directly or indirectly performed, as the common daylight and air, has no exchangeable value. That which requires the greatest amount of labor for its production, other things being equal, is most valuable. But there is as much mere physical capacity for labor dormant in a population of serfs and slaves, or of the subjects of an Oriental despotism, as in an equal population of the freest country on earth; as much in the same number of men in Asia Minor, or the Crimea, as in Yorkshire in England, or Middlesex in Massachusetts. But what a difference in the developments and applications of labor in the two classes of populations respectively! On the one hand, energy, fire, and endurance;on the other, languor and tardiness; on the one hand, a bold application of capital in giving employment to labor; on the other, a furtive concealment of capital where it exists, and a universal want of it for any new enterprise: on the one hand, artistic skill and moral courage superadded to the mere animal power of labor; on the other, every thing done by hand, in ancient, umimproving routine: on the one hand, a constantly increasing amount of skilled and energetic labor, resulting from the increase of a well-educated population; on the other hand, stationary, often declining numbers, and one generation hardly able to fill the place of its predecessor.

It is the spirit of a free country which animates and gives energy to its labor; which puts the mass in action, gives it motive and intensity, makes it inventive, sends it off in new directions, subdues to its command all the powers of nature, and enlists in its service an army of machines, that do all but think and talk. Compare a hand loom with a power loom; a barge, poled up against the current of a river, with a steamer breasting its force. The difference is not greater between them than between the efficiency of labor under a free or despotic government; in an independent state or a colony. I am disposed to think that the history of the world would concur with our own history, in proving that, in proportion as a community is under the full operation of the encouraging prospects and generous motives which exist in a free country, precisely in that proportion will its labor be efficient, enterprising, inventive, and productive of all the blessings of life.

This is a general operation of the establishment of an independent government in the United States of America, which has not perhaps been enough considered among us. We have looked too exclusively to the mere political change, and the substitution of a domestic for a foreign rule, as an historical fact, flattering to the national vanity. There was also another consequence of very great practical importance, which, in celebrating the declaration of independence at Lowell, ought not to pass unnoticed. While we were colonies of Great Britain, we were dependent on a government in which we were not represented. The laws passed by the Imperial Parliament were not passed for the benefit of the colony as their immediate object, but only so far as the interest of the colony was supposed to be consistent with that of the mother country. It was the principle of the colonial system of Europe, as it was administered before the revolution, to make the colonies subserve the growth and wealth of the parent state. The industry of the former was accordingly encouraged where it contributed to this object; it was discouraged and restrained where it was believed to have an opposite tendency. Hence the navigation law, by which the colonies were forbidden to trade directly with any but British ports. It is not easy to form a distinct conception of the paralyzing effect of such a restraint upon the industry of a population like ours, seated upon a coast which nature has indented with capacious harbors, and with a characteristic aptitude, from the earliest periods of our existence as a community, for maritime adventure.

The case was still worse in reference to manufactures. The climate of the northern and middle colonies is such as to make the manufacture of clothing one of the great concerns of civilized life. Apart from all views to the accumulation of wealth, the manufactures of wool, (and of late years of cotton,) of iron, leather, and wood, are connected with the comfortable subsistence of every family. And yet toall these branches of industry, except so far as they were carried on for household consumption, not only was no legislative favor extended by the home government, but they were from time to time made the subject of severe penal statutes. . . .

Accordingly, when the country entered upon the condition of independent political existence,. . . its manufacturing interests were suffering under the effect of a century of actual warfare, and the loss of all the skill which would have been acquired in a century's experience.

The establishment, therefore, of a prosperous manufacturing town like Lowell, regarded in itself, and as a specimen of other similar seats of American art and industry, may with propriety be considered as a peculiar triumph of our political independence. They are, if I may so express it, the complement of the revolution. They redress the peculiar hardships of the colonial system. They not only do that which was not done, but which was not permitted to be done before the establishment of an independent government. . .

I have thought it appropriate to the occasion to point out, in a summary way, the connection of the growth of our manufactures with the independence of the country; and I believe it would not be difficult to show that no event consequent upon the establishment of our independence, has been of greater public benefit.

Let us consider, first, the addition made to the capital of the country, by bringing into action the immense mechanical power which exists at the falls and rapids of our streams. Could the choice have been given to us, for the abode of our population, of a dead alluvial plain of twice the extent, every one feels that it would have been bad policy to accept the offer. Every one perceives that this natural water power is a vast accession to the wealth and capital of a state. The colonial system annihilated it, or, what was the same thing, prevented its application. To all practical purposes, it reduced the beautiful diversity of the surface—nature's grand and lovely landscape gardening of vale and mountain—to that dull alluvial level. The rivers broke over the rapids; but the voice of nature and Providence, which cried from them, "Let these be the seats of your creative industry," was uttered in vain. It was an element of prosperity which we held in unconscious possession. It is scarcely credible how completely the thoughts of men had been turned in a different direction. There is probably no country on the surface of the globe, of the same extent, on which a greater amount of this natural capital has been bestowed by Providence; but a century and a half passed by, not merely before it began to be profitably applied on a large scale, but before its existence even began to be suspected, and this in places where some of its greatest accumulations are found. If a very current impression in this community is not destitute of foundation, the site of Lowell was examined, no very long time before the commencement of the first factories here, and the report brought back was, that it presented no available water power. Does it not strike every one who hears me, that, in calling this water power into action, the country has gained just as much as it would by the gratuitous donation of the same amount of steam power; with the additional advantage in favor of the former, that it is, from the necessity of the case, far more widely distributed, stationed at salubrious spots, and unaccompanied with most of the disadvantages and evils incident to manufacturing establishments moved by steam in the crowded streets and unhealthy suburbs of large cities?

Of all this vast wealth bestowed upon the land by Providence,— brought into the common stock by the great partner Nature,—the colonial system, as I have observed, deprived us; and it is only since the establishment of our own manufactures that we have begun to turn it to account. Even now, the smallest part of it has been rendered available; and what has thus far been done is not so much important for its own sake as for pointing the way and

creating an inducement for further achievements in the same
direction. There is water power enough in the United States, as
yet unapplied, to sustain the industry of a population a hundred
fold as large as that now in existence. . . .

Connected with this is another benefit of the utmost importance,
and not wholly dissimilar in kind. The population gathered at a
manufacturing establishment is to be fed, and this gives an
enhanced value to the land in all the neighboring region. In this
new country the land often acquires a value in this way for the
first time. A large number of persons in this assembly are well able
to contrast the condition of the villages in the neighborhood of
Lowell with what it was ten or twelve years ago, when Lowell
itself consisted of two or three quite unproductive farms. It is the
contrast of production with barrenness; of cultivation with waste;
of plenty with an absence of every thing but the bare necessaries of
life. The effect, of course, in one locality is of no great account in
the sum of national production throughout the extent of the land.
But wherever a factory is established this effect is produced; and
every individual to whom they give employment ceases to be a
producer, and becomes a consumer of agricultural produce. The
aggregate effect is, of course, of the highest importance. . . .

There is another point of importance, in reference to manufactures, which ought not to be omitted in this connection, and it is
this—that in addition to what may be called their direct operation
and influence, manufactures are a great school for all the practical
arts. As they are aided themselves, in the progress of inventive
sagacity, by hints and materials from every art and every science,
and every kingdom of nature, so, in their turn, they create the skill
and furnish the instruments for carrying on almost all the other
pursuits. Whatever pertains to machinery, in all the great
branches of industry, will probably be found to have its origin,
directly or indirectly, in that skill which can be acquired only in
connection with manufactures. . . .

These important practical truths have been fully confirmed by
the experience of Lowell, where the most valuable improvements
have been made in almost every part of the machinery by which
its multifarious industry is carried on. But however interesting this
result may be, in an economical point of view, another lesson has
been taught at Lowell, and our other well-conducted manufacturing establishments, which I deem vastly more important. It is well
known that the degraded condition of the operatives in the old
world had created a strong prejudice against the introduction of

manufactures in this country. We were made acquainted, by sanitary and parliamentary reports, detailing the condition of the great manufacturing cities abroad, with a state of things revolting to humanity. It would seem that the industrial system of Europe required for its administration an amount of suffering, depravity, and brutalism, which formed one of the great scandals of the age. No form of serfdom or slavery could be worse. Reflecting persons, on this side of the ocean, contemplated with uneasiness the introduction, into this country, of a system which had disclosed such hideous features in Europe; but it must be frankly owned that these apprehensions have proved wholly unfounded. Were I addressing an audience in any other place, I could with truth say more to this effect than I will say on this occasion. But you will all bear me witness, that I do not speak the words of adulation when I say, that for physical comfort, moral conduct, general intelligence, and all the qualities of social character which make up an enlightened New England community, Lowell might safely enter into a comparison with any town or city in the land. Nowhere, I believe, for the same population, is there a greater number of schools and churches, and nowhere a greater number of persons whose habits and mode of life bear witness that they are influenced by a sense of character.

In demonstrating to the world that such a state of things is consistent with the profitable pursuit of manufacturing industry, you have made a discovery more important to humanity than all the wonderful machinery for weaving and spinning,—than all the miracles of water or steam. You have rolled off from the sacred cause of labor the mountain reproach of ignorance, vice, and suffering under which it lay crushed. You have gained, for the skilled industry required to carry on these mightly establishments, a place of honor in the great dispensation by which Providence governs the world. You have shown that the home-bred virtues of the parental roof are not required to be left behind by those who resort for a few years to these crowded marts of social industry; and, in the fruits of your honest and successful labor, you are daily carrying gladness to the firesides where you were reared. . . .

But it is time, fellow-citizens, that I should close. On Monday last, at the request of my friends and neighbors of Charlestown, I addressed them on the anniversary of the landing of Governor Winthrop, in 1630—the date, as it may with propriety be considered, of the effective settlement of Massachusetts. That was a day consecrated to hallowed recollections of olden times. We dwelt upon the sacrifices and privations of our ancestors while engaged, slowly and painfully, in laying the foundations upon which we have built. It is quite noticeable, that, within thirteen years from that time, the manufacture of cotton, of hemp, and of flax received considerable attention in this region; and that, as early as 1645, a legislative grant of very ample privileges, to encourage the manufacture of iron, was made to a company, headed by Governor Winthrop's son. Those were the days of faint and feeble beginnings. How different the train of associations awakened by the spot where we are now assembled! But ten years only ago, and Lowell did not exist; the soil on which it stands was an open field. These favored precincts, now resounding with all the voices of successful industry,—the abode of intelligent thousands,—lay hushed in the deep silence of nature, broken only by the unprofitable murmur of those streams which practical science and wisely applied capital have converted into the sources of its growth. The change seems more the work of enchantment than the regular progress of human agency. We can scarcely believe that we do not witness a great Arabian tale of real life; that a beneficent genius has not touched the soil with his wand, and caused a city to spring from its bosom. But it is not so. Your prosperous town is but another monument to the wisdom and patriotism of our fathers. It has grown up on the basis of the national independence. But for the deed which was done on the FOURTH OF JULY, 1776, your streets and squares would still be the sandy plain which nature made them.

PART TWO
An Age of Anxieties

5 FROM *James Kent*

No longer to Remain Plain and Simple Republics of Farmers

Traditionally, historians in evaluating the course of American history from the War of 1812 through the 1840s have based their interpretations on the doctrine of progress. The incredible economic and geographical expansion together with the innumerable optimistic writings of contemporaries seemed to give this view ample documentation. However, more recently scholars have uncovered convincing evidence of widespread uneasiness in expanding young America. On occasion, apprehensions took the form of a direct challenge to the whole concept of progress. Thoreau's Walden *was such a protest. More often, however, the anxieties of the period reveal themselves as covert fears underlying and clouding a progressive vision.*

The following selection is indicative of these covert fears. The speech of James Kent, Chancellor of the state of New York and an important figure in the development of an American legal system, ostensibly argued against the extension of the suffrage at the New York Constitutional Convention of 1821. In this respect, Kent's efforts (which were to no avail) could be considered as the last gasps of a dying Federalism. Yet implicit in Kent's speech is an ominous fear of the future. In the broadest sense, it was change itself that he dreaded. Like Jefferson, he believed that liberty and property could best be safeguarded by a population of freehold farmers. But, he saw around him the rise of commerce, manufactures, great cities, speculative capitalists, and a propertyless proletariat. His lament: "We stand, . . .this moment, on the

SOURCE. *Reports of the Proceedings and Debates of the Convention of 1821 ,* edited by Nathaniel H. Carter, William L. Stone, and Marcus T.C. Gould (Albany, 1821), pp. 219-222.

*brink of fate, on the very edge of the precipice," would be echoed time and
again in subsequent decades.*

I am in favor of the amendment which has been submitted by
my honourable colleague from Albany; and I must beg leave to
trespass for a few moments upon the patience of the committee,
while I state the reasons which have induced me to wish, that the
senate should continue, as heretofore, the representative of the
landed interest, and exempted from the control of universal
suffrage. I hope what I may have to say will be kindly received, for
it will be well intended. But, if I thought otherwise, I should still
prefer to hazard the loss of the little popularity which I might
have in this house, or out of it, than to hazard the loss of the
approbation of my own conscience.

I have reflected upon the report of the select committee with
attention and with anxiety. We appear to be disregarding the
principles of the constitution, under which we have so long and so
happily lived, and to be changing some of its essential institutions.
I cannot but think that the considerate men who have studied the
history of republics, or are read in lessons of experience, must look
with concern upon our apparent disposition to vibrate from a well
balanced government, to the extremes of the democratic doctrines.
Such a broad proposition as that contained in the report, at the
distance of ten years past, would have struck the public mind with
astonishment and terror. So rapid has been the career of our
vibration.

Let us recall our attention, for a moment, to our past history.

This state has existed for forty-four years under our present
constitution, which was formed by those illustrious sages and
patriots who adorned the revolution. It has wonderfully fulfilled
all the great ends of civil government. During that long period, we
have enjoyed in an eminent degree, the blessings of civil and
religious liberty. We have had our lives, our privileges, and our
property, protected. We have had a succession of wise and
temperate legislatures. The code of our statute law has been again
and again revised and corrected, and it may proudly bear a
comparison with that of any other people. We have had, during
that period, (though I am, perhaps, not the fittest person to say it)
a regular, stable, honest, and enlightened administration of justice.
All the peaceable pursuits of industry, and all the important

interests of education and science, have been fostered and encouraged. We have trebled our numbers within the last twenty-five years, have displayed mighty resources, and have made unexampled progress in the career of prosperity and greatness.

Our financial credit stands at an enviable height; and we are now successfully engaged in connecting the great lakes with the ocean by stupendous canals, which excite the admiration of our neighbours, and will make a conspicuous figure even upon the map of the United States.

These are some of the fruits of our present government; and yet we seem to be dissatisfied with our condition, and we are engaged in the bold and hazardous experiment of remoddelling the constitution. It is not fit and discreet: I speak as to wise men; is it not fit and proper that we should pause in our career, and reflect well on the immensity of the innovation in contemplation? Discontent in the midst of so much prosperity, and with such abundant means of happiness, looks like ingratitude, and as if we were disposed to arraign the goodness of Providence. Do we not expose ourselves to the danger of being deprived of the blessings we have enjoyed?— When the husbandman has gathered in his harvest, and has filled his barns and his graneries with the fruits of his industry, if he should then become discontented and unthankful, would he not have reason to apprehend, that the Lord of the harvest might come in his wrath, and with his lightening destroy them?

The senate has hitherto been elected by the farmers of the state—by the free and independent lords of the soil, worth at least $250 in freehold estate, over and above all debts charged thereon. The governor has been chosen by the same electors, and we have hitherto elected citizens of elevated rank and character. Our assembly has been chosen by freeholders, possessing a freehold of the value of $50 or by persons renting a tenement of the yearly value of $5, and who have been rated and actually paid taxes to the state. By the report before us, we propose to annihilate, at one stroke, all those property distinctions and to bow before the idol of universal suffrage. That extreme democratic principle, when applied to the legislative and executive departments of government, has been regarded with terror, by the wise men of every age, because in every European republic, ancient and modern, in which it has been tried, it has terminated disastrously, and been productive of corruption, injustice, violence, and tyranny. And dare we flatter ourselves that we are a peculiar people, who can run the career of history, exempted from the passions which have disturbed and corrupted the rest of mankind? If we are like other races of men, with similar follies and vices, then I greatly fear that our posterity will have reason to deplore in sackcloth and ashes, the delusion of the day.

It is not my purpose at present to interfere with the report of the committee, so far as respects the qualifications of electors for governor and members of assembly. I shall feel grateful if we may be permitted to retain the stability and security of a senate, bottomed upon the freehold property of the state. Such a body, so constituted, may prove a sheet anchor amidst the future factions and storms of the republic. The great leading and governing interest of this state, is, at present, the agricultural; and what madness would it be to commit that interest to the winds. The great body of the people, are now the owners and actual cultivators of the soil. With that wholesome population we always expect to find moderation, frugality, order, honesty, and a due sense of independence, liberty, and justice. It is impossible that any people can lose their liberties by internal fraud or violence, so long as the country is parcelled out among freeholders of moderate possessions, and those freeholders have a sure and efficient control in the affairs of the government. Their habits, sympathies, and employments, necessarily inspire them with a correct spirit of freedom and justice; they are the safest guardians of property and the laws: We certainly cannot too highly appreciate the value of the agricultural interest: It is the foundation of national wealth and power. According to the opinion of her ablest political economists, it is the surplus produce of the agriculture of England, that enables her to support her vast body of manufacturers, her formidable fleets and armies, and the crowds of persons engaged in the liberal professions, and the cultivation of the various arts.

Now, sir, I wish to preserve our senate as the representative of the landed interest. I wish those who have an interest in the soil, to retain the exclusive possession of a branch in the legislature, as a strong hold in which they may find safety through all the vicissitudes which the state may be destined, in the course of Providence, to experience. I wish them to be always enabled to say that their freeholds cannot be taxed without their consent. The men of no property, together with the crowds of dependants connected with great manufacturing and commercial establishments, and the motley and undefinable population of crowded ports, may, perhaps, at some future day, under skilful management, predominate in the assembly, and yet we should be perfectly safe if no laws could pass without the free consent of the owners of the soil. That security we at present enjoy; and it is that security which I wish to retain.

The apprehended danger from the experiment of universal suffrage applied to the whole legislative department, is no dream of the imagination. It is too mighty an excitement for the moral constitution of men to endure. The tendency of universal suffrage, is to jeopardize the rights of property, and the principles of liberty. There is a constant tendency in human society, and the history of every age proves it; there is a tendency in the poor to covet and to share the plunder of the rich; in the debtor to relax or avoid the obligation of contracts; in the majority to tyranize over the minority, and trample down their rights; in the indolent and the profligate, to cast the whole burthens of society upon the industrious and the virtuous; and *there is a tendency in ambitious and wicked men, to inflame these combustible materials.* It requires a vigilant government, and a firm administration of justice, to counteract that tendency. Thou shalt not covet; thou shalt not steal; are divine injunctions induced by this miserable depravity of our nature. Who can undertake to calculate with any precision, how many millions of people, this great state will contain in the course of this and the next century, and who can estimate the future extent and magnitude of our commercial ports? The disproportion between the men of property, and the men of no property, will be in every society in a ratio to its commerce, wealth, and population. We are no longer to remain plain and simple republics of farmers, like the New-England colonists, or the Dutch settlements on the Hudson. We are fast becoming a great nation, with great commerce, manufactures, population, wealth, luxuries, and with the vices and miseries that they engender. One seventh of the population of the city of Paris at this day subsists on charity, and one third of the inhabitants of that city die in the hospitals; what would become of such a city with universal suffrage? France has upwards of four, and England upwards of five millions of manufacturing and commercial labourers without property. Could these kingdoms sustain the weight of universal suffrage? The radicals in England, with the force of that mighty engine, would at once sweep away the property, the laws, and the liberties of that island like a deluge.

The growth of the city of New-York is enough to startle and awaken those who are pursuing the *ignis fatuus* of universal suffrage.

In 1773 it had 21,000 souls.
    1801 it had 60,000 do.
    1806 it had 60,000 do.
    1820 it had 123,000 do.

It is rapidly swelling into the unwieldly population, and with the burdensome pauperism, of an European metropolis. New-York is destined to become the future London of America; and in less than a century, that city, with the operation of universal suffrage, and under skilful direction, will govern this state.

The notion that every man that works a day on the road, or serves an idle hour in the militia, is entitled as of right to an equal participation in the whole power of the government, is most unreasonable, and has no foundation in justice. We had better at once discard from the report such a nominal test of merit. If such persons have an equal share in one branch of the legislature, it is surely as much as they can in justice or policy demand. Society is an association for the protection of property as well as of life, and the individual who contributes only one cent to the common stock, ought not to have the same power and influence in directing the property concerns of the partnership, as he who contributes his thousands. He will not have the same inducements to care, and diligence, and fidelity. His inducements and his temptation would be to divide the whole capital upon the principles of an agrarian law.

Liberty, rightly understood, is an inestimable blessing, but liberty without wisdom, and without justice, is no better than wild and savage licentiousness. The danger which we have hereafter to apprehend, is not the want, but the abuse, of liberty. We have to apprehend the oppression of minorities, and a disposition to encroach on private right—to disturb chartered privileges—and to weaken, degrade, and overawe the administration of justice; we have to apprehend the establishment of unequal, and consequently, unjust systems of taxation, and all the mischiefs of a crude and mutable legislation. A stable senate, exempted from the influence of universal suffrage, will powerfully check these dangerous propensities, and such a check becomes the more necessary, since this Convention has already determined to withdraw the watchful eye of the judicial department from the passage of laws.

We are destined to become a great manufacturing as well as commercial state. We have already numerous and prosperous factories of one kind or another, and one master capitalist with his one hundred apprentices, and journeymen, and agents, and dependents, will bear down at the polls, an equal number of farmers of small estates in his vicinity, who cannot safely unite for their common defence. Large manufacturing and mechanical establishments, can act in an instant with the unity and efficacy of disciplined troops. It is against such combinations, among others, that I think we ought to give to the freeholders, or those who have interest in land, one branch of the legislature for their asylum and their comfort. Universal suffrage once granted, is granted forever, and never can be recalled. There is no retrograde step in the rear of democracy. However mischievous the precedent may be in its consequences, or however fatal in its effects, universal suffrage never can be recalled or checked, but by the strength of the bayonet. We stand, therefore, this moment, on the brink of fate, on the very edge of the precipice. If we let go our present hold on the senate, we commit our proudest hopes and our most precious interests to the waves.

It ought further to be observed, that the senate is a court of justice in the last resort. It is the last depository of public and private rights; of civil and criminal justice. This gives the subject an awful consideration, and wonderfully increases the importance of securing that house from the inroads of universal suffrage. Our country freeholders are exclusively our jurors in the administration of justice, and there is equal reason that none but those who have an interest in the soil, should have any concern in the composition of that court. As long as the senate is safe, justice is safe, property is safe, and our liberties are safe. But when the wisdom, the integrity, and the independence of that court is lost, we may be certain that the freedom and happiness of this state, are fled forever.

I hope, sir, we shall not carry desolation through all the departments of the fabric erected by our fathers. I hope we shall not put forward to the world a new constitution, as will meet with the scorn of the wise, and the tears of the patriot.

6 FROM

Leo Marx
The Machine in the Garden

James Kent's sense that mechanization was creating a violent break with America's pastoral past was not an uncommon attitude. In the following article, Leo Marx, a professor of American studies at Amherst College, points out that the literary generation of Emerson and Hawthorne was particularly sensitive to the tensions caused by the sudden thrust of the machine into the garden of agrarian America. At base, the conflict was between two concepts of man and his relationship to the universe. The traditional agrarian view suggested a passive and organic relationship in which man lived in harmony with nature. The technological view, on the other hand, implied an active and assertive dominance over nature through machine power. Almost to a man, the great writers of the Jacksonian generation opposed the triumph of technology as an aesthetic and moral violation of nature.

> . . .*the artist must employ the symbols in use in his day and nation to convey his enlarged sense to his fellow-men.*
>
> RALPH WALDO EMERSON

I.

The response of American writers to industrialism has been a typical and, in many respects, a distinguishing feature of our culture. The Industrial Revolution, of course, was international, but certain aspects of the process were intensified in this country. Here, for one thing, the Revolution was delayed, and when it began it was abrupt, thorough, and dramatic. During a decisive phase of that transition, our first significant literary generation, that of Hawthorne and Emerson, came to maturity. Hence it may be said that our literature, virtually from the beginning, has embodied the experience of a people crossing the line which sets off the era of machine production from the rest of human history. As

SOURCE. Leo Marx, "The Machine in the Garden," *The New England Quarterly*, XXIX, Number 1 (March 1956), pp. 27-42.

Emerson said, speaking of the century as the "age of tools," so many inventions had been added in his time that life seemed "almost made over new." This essay demonstrates one of the ways in which a sense of the transformation of life by the machine has contributed to the temper of our literature. The emphasis is upon the years before 1860, because the themes and images with which our major writers then responded to the onset of the Machine Age have provided us with a continuing source of meaning.

Some will justifiably object, however, that very little of the work of Emerson, Thoreau, Hawthorne, or Melville actually was *about* the Industrial Revolution. But this fact hardly disposes of the inquiry; indeed, one appeal of the subject is precisely the need to meet this objection. For among the many arid notions which have beset inquiries into the relations between literature and society, perhaps the most barren has been the assumption that artists respond to history chiefly by making history their manifest subject. As if one might adequately gauge the imaginative impact of atomic power by seeking out direct allusions to it in recent literature. Our historical scholars do not sufficiently distinguish between the setting of a literary work (it may be institutional, geographical, or historical) and its subject-matter or theme. A poem set in a factory need be no more about industrialism than *Hamlet* about living in castles. Not that the setting is without significance. But the first obligation of the scholar, like any other reader of literature, is to know what the work is about. Only then may he proceed to his special business of elucidating the relevance of the theme to the experience of the age.

But here a difficulty arises: the theme itself cannot be said to "belong" to the age. It is centuries old. The Promethean theme, for example, belongs to no single time or place; history periodically renews man's sense of the perils attendant upon the conquest of nature. This obvious fact lends force to the view, tacit postulate of much recent criticism, that what we value in art derives from (and resides in) a realm beyond time, or, for that matter, society. Yet because the scholar grants his inability to account for the genesis of themes, he need not entertain a denial of history. True, he should not speak, for example, of *the* literature of industrialism, as if there were serious works whose controlling insights originate in a single, specific historical setting. But he has every reason to assume that certain themes and conventions, though they derive from the remote past, may have had a peculiar relevance to an age suddenly aware that machines were making life over new. That, in any case, is what seems to have happened in the age of Emerson and Melville. Because our writers seldom employed industrial settings until late in the century we have throught that only then did the prospect of a mechanized America affect their vision of life. My view is that an awareness of the Machine Revolution has been vital to our literature since the eighteen thirties.

But what of a man like Hawthorne, whom we still regard as the "pure" artist, and whose work apparently bears little relation to the Industrial Revolution of his age? In his case it is necessary to demonstrate the importance for his work of matters about which he wrote virtually nothing. Here is "Ethan Brand," a characteristic story developed from an idea Hawthorne recorded in 1843: "The search of an investigator for the Unpardonable Sin;—he at last finds it in his own heart and practice." The theme manifestly has nothing to do with industrialization. On the contrary, it is traditional; we correctly associate it with the Faust myth. Nevertheless, some facts about the genesis of the tale are suggestive. For its physical details, including characters and landscape, Hawthorne drew upon notes he had made during a Berkshire vacation in 1838. At that time several new factories were in operation along the mountain streams near North Adams. He was struck by the sight of machinery in the green hills; he took elaborate notes, and conceived the idea of a malignant steam engine which attacked and killed its human attendants. But he did nothing with that idea, or with any of his other observations upon the industrialization of the Berkshires. And the fact remains that nowhere, in "Ethan Brand" or the notebooks, do we find any explicit evidence of a direct link between Hawthorne's awareness of the new power and this fable of the quest for knowledge of absolute evil.

II.

Nevertheless this connection can, I believe, be established. What enables us to establish it is the discovery of a body of imagery through which the age repeatedly expressed its response to the Industrial Revolution. This "imagery of technology" is decisively present in "Ethan Brand."

Although the theme is traditional, some components of the tale take on their full significance only when we consider what was happening in America at the time. Between 1830 and 1860 the image of the machine, and the idea of a society founded upon machine power suddenly took hold of the public imagination. In the magazines, for example, images of industrialism, and particularly images associated with the power of steam, were widely employed as emblems of America's future. They stood for progress, productivity, and, above all, man's new power over nature. And they invariably carried a sense of violent break with the past. Later, looking back at those years, Henry Adams compressed the essential feeling into his account of the way "he and his eighteenth century. . . were suddenly cut apart—separated forever. . ." by the railroad, steamship, and telegraph. It is the suddenness and finality of change—the recent past all at once a green colonial memory—to which American writers have persistently called attention. The motif recurs in our literature from *Walden* to *The Bear.*

But at first our writers did not respond by writing *about* the Industrial Revolution. Long before they knew enough to find concepts for the experience, as Adams later could do, they had invested their work with ideas and emotions it provoked. To this end they drew upon images of technology already familiar to the public. Such collective representations, or "cultural images," allowed them to express what they could not yet fully understand. And at times they heightened these images to the intensity of symbols. The symbolism of Hawthorne and Melville was, after all, designed to get at circumstances which gave rise to conflicting emotions, and which exceeded, in their complexity, the capacities of understanding. Indeed, there is reason to believe that the unprecedented changes then taking place may have provided a direct impetus to the use of symbolic techniques. Hawthorne admitted as much in explaining why he required the image of the railroad to convey that sense of loneliness in the crowd he thought characteristic of the new America. This image, he said, enabled him to present the feeling of a "whole world, both morally and physically,. . . detached from its old standfasts and set in rapid motion."

Now, as the statements of Emerson, Adams, and Hawthorne suggest, the evocative power of the imagery of industrialism is not to be attributed to any intrinsic feature of machines. What gives rise to the emotion is not the machine, but rather its presence against the felt background of the older historic landscape. The American landscape, in fact, accounts for another singular feature of the response to our Industrial Revolution. In this country mechanization had been arrested, among other things, by space— the sheer extent of the land itself. Then, suddenly, with the application of the energy of heat to transport, this obstacle had been overcome. Hence the dramatic decisiveness of the changes in Hawthorne's time, when steam power was suddenly joined to the forces already pressing to occupy the virgin land. In America machines were preeminently conquerors of nature-nature conceived as space. They blazed across a raw landscape of wilderness and farm.

Now it is hardly necessary to discuss the high value, esthetic, moral, and even political, with which the landscape had so recently been invested. Henry Nash Smith has indicated how central a place images of the landscape occupied in the popular vision of America's future as new Garden of the World. The sudden appearance of the Machine in the Garden deeply stirred an age already sensitive to the conflict between civilization and nature. This symbolic tableau recorded the tension between two opposed conceptions of man's relations with his universe. The society prefigured by the myth of the Garden would celebrate a passive accommodation to nature's law. There, survival would depend upon organic production or growth. But, on the other hand, the machine foretold an economy designed by man's brain, and it implied an active, indeed proud, assertion of his dominion over nature. Hence the writers of the American "renaissance," not unlike Shakespeare's contemporaries, confronted one of the more rewarding situations history bestows upon art: the simultaneous attraction of two visions of a people's destiny, each embodying a discrete view of human experience, and each, moreover, accompanied by fresh and vivid symbols. The theme was as old as the story of Prometheus and Epimetheus, but its renewed vitality in Hawthorne's day may be attributed to the power with which fire was making life over new.

III.

In 1838, five years before Hawthorne had formulated the moral germ of "Ethan Brand," he had been struck by an actual sight of this change in American society. "And taking a turn in the road," he wrote, "behold these factories. . . .And perhaps the wild scenery is all around the very site of the factory and mingles its impression strangely with those opposite ones." Here was history made visible. What most impressed Hawthorne was a "sort of picturesqueness in finding these factories, supremely artificial establishments, in the midst of such wild scenery." Nevertheless, ten years later, when Hawthorne so thoroughly mined this

Berkshire notebook for "Ethan Brand," he passed over these impressions. The factories do not appear in the story. Nor is there any overt allusion to industrialization. To speculate about the reasons for this "omission" would take us far afield. Whatever the reason, the important fact is not that "Ethan Brand" contains no mention of the factories themselves, but that the ideas and emotions they suggested to Hawthorne are central to the story.

A sense of loss, anxiety, and dislocation hangs over the world of "Ethan Brand." The mood is located in the landscape. At the outset we hear that the countryside is filled with "relics of antiquity." What caused this melancholy situation becomes apparent when Hawthorne describes the people of the region. Brand has returned from his quest. Word is sent to the village, and a crowd climbs the mountain to hear his tale. From among them Hawthorne singles out several men: the stage-agent, recently deprived of his vocation; an old-fashioned country doctor, his useful days gone by; and a man who has lost a hand (emblem of craftsmanship?) in the "devilish grip of a steam-engine". He is now a "fragment of a human being." Like the Wandering Jew and the forlorn old man who searches for his lost daughter (said to have been a victim of Ethan's experimental bent), all are derelicts. They are victims of the fires of change. Like the monomaniac hero himself, all suffer a sense of not belonging.

This intense feeling of "unrelatedness" to nature and society has often been ascribed to the very historical forces which Hawthorne had observed in 1838. Discussing the intellectual climate of that era, Emerson once remarked that young men then had been born with knives in their brains. This condition was a result, he said, of the pervasive "war between intellect and affection." He called it "detachment," and found it reflected everywhere in the age; in Kant, Goethe's *Faustt,* and in the consequences of the new capitalist power. "Instead of the social existence which all shared," he wrote, "was now separation." Whatever we choose to call it—"detachment" or "alienation" (Karl Marx), or "anomie" (Emile Durkheim) or "dissociation of sensibility" (T.S. Eliot)—this is the malaise from which Ethan suffered. Though there are important differences of emphasis, each of these terms refers to the state of mind of an individual cut off from a realm of experience said to be an indispensable source of life's meaning. The source may vary, but it is significant that the responsible agent, or *separator,* so to speak, is invariably identified with science or industrial technology. In this sense Hawthorne's major theme was as vividly contemporary as it was traditional. He gave us the classic American account of the anguish of detachment.

The knife in Ethan's brain was a "cold philosophical curiosity" which led to a "separation of the intellect from the heart." Now it is of the utmost significance that this scientific obsession is said to have literally emanated from the fire. There was a legend about Ethan's having been accustomed "to evoke a fiend from the hot furnace". Together they spent many nights by the fire evolving the idea of the quest. But the fiend always retreated through the "iron door" of the kiln with the first glimmer of sunlight. Here we discover how Hawthorne's earlier impressions of industrialization have been transmuted in the creative process. Here is the conduit through which thought and emotion flow to the work from the artist's experience of his age. In this case the symbolic contrast between fire and sun serves the purpose. It blends a traditional convention (we think of Milton's Hell) and immediate experience; it provides the symbolic frame for the entire story. "Ethan Brand" begins at sundown and ends at dawn. During the long night the action centers upon the kiln or "furnace" which replaces the sun as source of warmth, light, and (indirectly) sustenance. The fire in the kiln is at once the symbolic source of evil and of the energy necessary to make nature's raw materials useful to man. Moreover, it can be shown that the very words and phrases used to describe this fire are used elsewhere, by Hawthorne, in direct reference to industrialization. In the magazines of the day fire was repeatedly identified with the new machine power. Hence fire, whatever its traditional connotations, is here an emblem, or fragment of an emblem, of the nascent industrial order. The new America was being forged by fire.

But if fire cripples men and devastates the landscape in "Ethan Brand," the sun finally dispels anxiety and evil, restoring man's solidarity with nature. When Ethan dies, his body burned to a brand by the satanic flames which had possessed his soul, the fire goes out and the ravaged landscape disappears. In its stead we see a golden vision of the self-contained New England village. The sun is just coming up. The hills swell gently about the town, as if resting "peacefully in the hollow of the great hand of Providence." In pointed contrast to the murky atmosphere of Ethan's Walpur-gisnacht, there is no smoke anywhere. The sun allows perfect clarity of perception. Every house is "distinctly visible." At the center of this pastoral tableau the spires of the churches catch the first rays of the sun. Now the countryside is invested with all the order and serenity and permanence which the fire had banished. This harmony between man and nature is then projected beyond time in the vision of a stepladder of clouds on which it seemed that (from such a social order?) "mortal man might thus ascend into heavenly regions." Finally, though he had already hinted that stage coaches were obsolete, Hawthorne introduces one into this eighteenth-century New England version of the Garden of Eden.

Beneath the surface of "Ethan Brand" we thus find many of the ideas and emotions aroused by the Machine's sudden entrance into the Garden. But this is not to say that the story is *about* industrialization. It is about the consequences of breaking the magic chain of humanity. That is the manifest theme and, like the symbols through which it is developed, the theme is traditional. His apprehension of the tradition permits Hawthorne to discover meanings in contemporary facts. On the other hand, the capacity of this theme and these images to excite the imagination must also be ascribed to their vivid relevance to life in modern America. This story, in short, is an amalgam of tradition, which supplies the theme, and experience, which presents the occasion, and imagery common to both.

IV.

But it may be said that, after all, this is merely one short story. The fact remains, however, that the same, or related, images may be traced outward from this story to Hawthorne's other work, the work of his contemporaries, the work of many later writers, and the society at large.

It is revealing, for example, that Hawthorne so often described his villains as alchemists, thereby associating them with fire and smoke. We recall that Aylmer, the scientist in "The Birthmark," made a point of building his laboratory underground to avoid sunlight. Or consider Rappaccini, whose experiments perverted the Garden itself. His flowers were evil because of their "artificialness indicating. . .the production. . .no longer of God's making, but the monstrous offspring of man's depraved fancy. . . ." From Hamilton's "Report on Manufactures" in 1791 until today, American thinking about industrialism, in and out of literature, has been tangled in the invidious distinction between "artificial" and "natural" production. These adjectives, like so much of American political rhetoric, along with Hawthorne's theme of isolation, are a characteristic legacy of agrarian experience. They are expressions of our native tradition of pastoral, with its glorification of the Garden and its consequent identification of science and technology with evil. To Hawthorne's contemporaries, Emerson, Thoreau, and Whitman, the sun also represented the primal source of redemption. "The sun rose clear," Thoreau tells us at the beginning of *Walden;* though he notes that the smoke of the train momentarily obscures its rays, the book ends with a passionate affirmation of the possibility of renewed access, as in "Ethan Brand," to its redeeming light: "The sun is but a morning star."

In *Moby-Dick*, published three years after "Ethan Brand," the identical motif emerges as a controlling element of tragedy. The "Try-Works," a crucial chapter in Ishmael's progressive renunciation of Ahab's quest, is quite literally constructed out of the symbols of "Ethan Brand." Again it is night, and vision is limited to the lurid light of a "kiln" or "furnace." Fire again is a means of production, rendering the whale's fat, and again it is also the source of alienation. Ishmael, at the helm, controls the ship's fate. Like Ethan he momentarily succumbs to the enchantment of fire, and so nearly fulfills Ahab's destructive destiny. But he recovers his sanity in time, and tells us: "Look not too long in the face of the fire, O Man! . . .believe not the *artificial fire* when its redness makes all things look ghastly. Tomorrow, in the *natural sun*, the skies will be bright; those who glared like devils in the forking flames, the more will show in far other, at least gentler relief; the glorious, golden, glad sun, the only true lamp—all others but liars!"

From this passage we may trace lines of iconological continuity to the heart of Melville's meaning. When the *Pequod* sailed both Ahab and Ishmael suffered the pain of "detachment." But if the voyage merely reinforced Ahab's worship of the power of fire, it provoked in Ishmael a reaffirmation of the Garden. Ahab again and again expressed his aspiration in images of fire and iron, cogs and wheels, automata, and manufactured men. He had his "humanities," and at times was tempted by thoughts of "green land," but Ahab could not finally renounce the chase. In *Moby-Dick* space is the sea—a sea repeatedly depicted in images of the American landscape. The conquest of the whale was a type of our fated conquest of nature itself. But in the end Ishmael in effect renounced the fiery quest. He was cured and saved. His rediscovery of that pastoral accommodation to the mystery of growth and fertility was as vital to his salvation as it had been to the myth of the Garden. The close identity of the great democratic God and the God of the Garden was a central facet of Melville's apocalyptic insight.

His was also a tragic insight. Ahab and Ishmael, representing irreconcilable conceptions of America's destiny, as indeed of all human experience, were equally incapable of saving the *Pequod.* From Melville to Faulkner our writers have provided a desperate recognition of this truth: of the attributes necessary for survival, the Ahabs alone have been endowed with the power, and the Ishmaels with the perception. Ishmael was saved. But like one of Job's messengers, he was saved to warn us of greater disasters in store for worshippers of fire. In this way imagery associated with the Machine's entrance into the Garden has served to join native experience and inherited wisdom.

7   FROM   *Nathaniel Hawthorne*
The Celestial Railroad

Leo Marx's analysis of Hawthorne's "Ethan Brand" in the previous article argued that even in a story not directly about industrialization or technology the conflict between the machine and the garden was implicit. If anyone questions Marx's interpretation of Hawthorne, however, the following short story, The Celestial Railroad, *should make clear the latter's apprehensions about the technological shortcut to progress that most Americans seemed bent on following. Published in 1843, this updated* Pilgrim's Progress *clearly shows the romantic writer's doubts about the direction in which America's material advance was leading.*

Not a great while ago, passing through the gate of dreams, I visited that region of the earth in which lies the famous City of Destruction. It interested me much to learn that by the public

SOURCE. Nathaniel Hawthorne, *Mosses From an Old Manse* (Boston, Houghton, Mifflin and Company, 1881), pp. 216-239.

spirit of some of the inhabitants a railroad has recently been established between this populous and flourishing town and the Celestial City. Having a little time upon my hands, I resolved to gratify a liberal curiosity by making a trip thither. Accordingly, one fine morning after paying my bill at the hotel and directing the porter to stow my luggage behind a coach, I took my seat in the vehicle and set out for the station house. It was my good fortune to enjoy the company of a gentleman—one Mr. Smooth-it-away—who, though he had never actually visited the Celestial City, yet seemed as well acquainted with its laws, customs, policy, and statistics as with those of the City of Destruction, of which he was a native townsman. Being moreover a director of the railroad corporation and one of its largest stockholders, he had it in his power to give me all desirable information respecting that praiseworthy enterprise.

Our coach rattled out of the city, and at a short distance from its outskirts passed over a bridge of elegant construction, but somewhat too slight, as I imagined, to sustain any considerable weight. On both sides lay an extensive quagmire, which could not have been more disagreeable, either to sight or smell, had all the kennels of the earth emptied their pollution there.

"This," remarked Mr. Smooth-it-away, "is the famous Slough of Despond—a disgrace to all the neighborhood; and the greater, that it might so easily be converted into firm ground."

"I have understood," said I, "that efforts have been made for that purpose from time immemorial. Bunyan mentions that above twenty thousand cartloads of wholesome instructions had been thrown in here without effect."

"Very probably! And what effect could be anticipated from such unsubstantial stuff?" cried Mr. Smooth-it-away. "You observe this convenient bridge. We obtained a sufficient foundation for it by throwing into the slough some editions of books of morality; volumes of French philosophy and German rationalism, tracts, sermons, and essays of modern clergymen; extracts from Plato, Confucius, and various Hindoo sages, together with a few ingenious commentaries upon texts of Scripture,—all of which, by some scientific process, have been converted into a mass like granite. The whole bog might be filled up with similar matter."

It really seemed to me, however, that the bridge vibrated and heaved up and down in a very formidable manner; and, spite of Mr. Smooth-it-away's testimony to the solidity of its foundation, I should be loath to cross it in a crowded omnibus, especially if each passenger; were encumbered with as heavy luggage as that gentleman and myself. Nevertheless we got over without accident, and soon found ourselves at the station house. . . .

A large number of passengers were already at the station house awaiting the departure of the cars. By the aspect and demeanor of these persons it was easy to judge that the feelings of the community had undergone a very favorable change in reference to the celestial pilgrimage. It would have done Bunyan's heart good to see it. Instead of a lonely and ragged man with a huge burden on his back, plodding along sorrowfully on foot while the whole city hooted after him here were parties of the first gentry and most respectable people in the neighborhood setting forth towards the Celestial City as cheerfully as if the pilgrimage were merely a summer tour. Among the gentlemen were characters of deserved eminence—magistrates, politicians, and men of wealth, by whose example religion could not but be greatly recommended to their meaner brethren. In the ladies' apartment, too, I rejoiced to distinguish some of those flowers of fashionable society who are so well fitted to adorn the most elevated circles of the Celestial City. There was much pleasant conversation about the news of the day, topics of business, and politics, or the lighter matters of amusement; while religion, though indubitably the main thing at heart, was thrown tastefully into the background. Even an infidel would have heard little or nothing to shock his sensibility.

One great convenience of the new method of going on pilgrimage I must not forget to mention. Our enormous burdens, instead of being carried on our shoulders as had been the custom of old, were all snugly deposited in the baggage car, and, as I was assured, would be delivered to their respective owners at the journey's end. . . .

The engine at this moment took its station in advance of the cars, looking, I must confess, much more like a sort of mechanical demon that would hurry us to the infernal regions than a laudable contrivance for smoothing our way to the Celestial City. On its top sat a personage almost enveloped in smoke and flame, which not to startle the reader, appeared to gush from his own mouth and stomach as well as from the engine's brazen abdomen. . . .

The passengers being all comfortably seated, we now rattled away merrily, accomplishing a greater distance in ten minutes than Christian probably trudged over in a day. It was laughable, while we glanced along, as it were, at the tail of a thunderbolt, to observe two dusty foot travellers in the old pilgrim guise, with cockle shell and staff, their mystic rolls of parchment in their hands and their intolerable burdens on their backs. The preposterous obstinacy of these honest people in persisting to groan and stumble along the difficult pathway rather than take advantage of modern improvements, excited great mirth among our wiser brotherhood. We greeted the two pilgrims with many pleasant gibes and a roar of laughter; whereupon they gazed at us with such woeful and absurdly compassionate visages that our merriment grew tenfold more obstreperous. . . .

Before our talk on this subject came to a conclusion we were rushing by the place where Christian's burden fell from his shoulders at the sight of the Cross. This served as a theme for Mr. Smooth-it-away, Mr. Live-for-the-world, Mr. Hide-sin-in-the-heart, Mr. Scaly-conscience, and a knot of gentlemen from the town of Shun-repentance, to descant upon the inestimable advantages resulting from the safety of our baggage. Myself, and all the passengers indeed, joined with great unanimity in this view of the matter; for our burdens were rich in many things esteemed precious throughout the world; and, especially, we each of us possessed a great variety of favorite Habits, which we trusted would not be out of fashion even in the polite circles of the Celestial City. It would have been a sad spectacle to see such an assortment of valuable articles tumbling into the sepulchre. Thus pleasantly conversing on the favorable circumstances of our position as compared with those of past pilgrims and of narrow minded ones at the present day, we soon found ourselves at the foot of the Hill Difficulty. Through the very heart of this rocky mountain a tunnel has been constructed of most admirable architecture, with a lofty arch and a spacious double track; so that, unless the earth and rocks should chance to crumble down, it will remain an eternal monument of the builder's skill and enterprise. It is a great though incidental advantage that the materials from the heart of the Hill Difficulty have been employed in filling up the Valley of Humiliation, thus obviating the necessity of descending into that disagreeable and unwholesome hollow. . . .

Consulting Mr. Bunyan's road book, I perceived that we must now be within a few miles of the Valley of the Shadow of Death, into which doleful region, at our present speed, we should plunge much sooner than seemed at all desirable. In truth, I expected nothing better than to find myself in the ditch on one side or the quag on the other; but on communicating my apprehensions to

Mr. Smooth-it-away, he assured me that the difficulties of this passage, even in its worst condition, had been vastly exaggerated, and that, in its present state of improvement, I might consider myself as safe as on any railroad in Christendom.

Even while we were speaking the train shot into the entrance of this dreaded Valley. Though I plead guilty to some foolish palpitations of the heart during our headlong rush over the causeway here constructed, yet it were unjust to withhold the highest encomiums on the boldness of its original conception and the ingenuity of those who executed it. It was gratifying, likewise, to observe how much care had been taken to dispel the everlasting gloom and supply the defect of cheerful sunshine, not a ray of which has ever penetrated among these awful shadows. For this purpose, the inflammable gas which exudes plentifully from the soil is collected by means of pipes, and thence communicated to a quadruple row of lamps along the whole extent of the passage. Thus a radiance has been created even out of the fiery and sulphurous curse that rests forever upon the valley—a radiance hurtful, however, to the eyes, and somewhat bewildering, as I discovered by the changes which it wrought in the visages of my companions. In this respect, as compared with natural daylight, there is the same difference as between truth and falsehood; but if the reader have ever travelled through the dark Valley, he will have learned to be thankful for any light that he could get—if not from the sky above, then from the blasted soil beneath. Such was the red brilliancy of these lamps that they appeared to build walls of fire on both sides of the track, between which we held our course at lightning speed, while a reverberating thunder filled the Valley with its echoes. Had the engine run off the track—a catastrophe, it is whispered, by no means unprecedented,—the bottomless pit, if there be any such place, would undoubtedly have received us. Just as some dismal fooleries of this nature had made my heart quake there came a tremendous shriek, careering along the valley as if a thousand devils had burst their lungs to utter it, but which proved to be merely the whistle of the engine on arriving at a stopping place.

The spot where we had now paused is the same that our friend Bunyan—a truthful man, but infected with many fantastic notions—has designated, in terms plainer than I like to repeat, as the mouth of the infernal region. This, however, must be a mistake, inasmuch as Mr. Smooth-it-away, while we remained in the smoky and lurid cavern, took occasion to prove that Tophet has not even a metaphorical existence. The place, he assured us, is no other than the crater of a half-extinct volcano, in which the directors had caused forges to be set up for the manufacture of railroad iron. Hence, also, is obtained a plentiful supply of fuel for the use of the engines. Whoever had gazed into the dismal obscurity of the broad cavern mouth, whence ever and anon darted huge tongues of dusky flame, and had seen the strange, half-shaped monsters, and visions of faces horribly grotesque, into which the smoke seemed to wreathe itself, and had heard the awful murmurs, and shrieks, and deep, shuddering whispers of the blast, sometimes forming themselves into words almost articulate, would have seized upon Mr. Smooth-it-away's comfortable explanation as greedily as we did. The inhabitants of the cavern, moreover, were unlovely personages, dark, smoke-begrimed, generally deformed, with misshapen feet, and a glow of dusky redness in their eyes as if their hearts had caught fire and were blazing out of the upper windows. It struck me as a peculiarity that the laborers at the forge and those who brought fuel to the engine, when they began to draw short breath, positively emitted smoke from their mouth and nostrils. . . .

Rattling onward through the Valley, we were dazzled with the fiercely gleaming gas lamps, as before. But sometimes, in the dark of intense brightness, grim faces, that bore the aspect and expression of individual sins, or evil passions, seemed to thrust themselves through the veil of light, glaring upon us, and stretching forth a great, dusky hand, as if to impede our progress. I almost thought that they were my own sins that appalled me there. These were freaks of imagination—nothing more, certainly—mere delusions, which I ought to be heartily ashamed of; but all through the Dark Valley I was tormented, and pestered, and dolefully bewildered with the same kind of waking dreams. The mephitic gases of that region intoxicate the brain. As the light of natural day, however, began to struggle with the glow of the lanterns, these vain imaginations lost their vividness, and finally vanished with the first ray of sunshine that greeted our escape from the Valley of the Shadow of Death. Ere we had gone a mile beyond it I could well nigh have taken my oath that this whole gloomy passage was a dream.

At the end of the valley, as John Bunyan mentions, is a cavern, where, in his days, dwelt two cruel giants, Pope and Pagan, who had strown the ground about their residence with the bones of slaughtered pilgrims. These vile old troglodytes are no longer there; but into their deserted cave another terrible giant has thrust himself, and makes it his business to seize upon honest travellers and fatten them for his table with plentiful meals of smoke, mist, moonshine, raw potatoes, and sawdust. He is a German by birth, and is called Giant Transcendentalist; but as to his form, his features, his substance, and his nature generally, it is the chief peculiarity of this huge miscreant that neither he for himself, nor any body for him, has ever been able to describe them. As we rushed by the cavern's mouth we caught a hasty glimpse of him, looking somewhat like an ill-proportioned figure, but considerably more like a heap of fog and duskiness. He shouted after us, but in so strange a phraseology that we knew not what he meant, nor whether to be encouraged or affrighted.

It was late in the day when the train thundered into the ancient city of Vanity, where Vanity Fair is still at the height of prosperity, and exhibits an epitome of whatever is brilliant, gay, and fascinating beneath the sun. . . .Many passengers stop to take their pleasure or make their profit in the Fair, instead of going onward to the Celestial City. . . .

Finally, after a pretty long residence at the Fair, I resumed my journey towards the Celestial City, still with Mr. Smooth-it-away at my side. At a short distance beyond the suburbs of Vanity we passed the ancient silver mine, of which Demas was the first discoverer, and which is now wrought to great advantage, supplying nearly all the coined currency of the world. . . .

The road now plunged into a gorge of the Delectable Mountains, and traversed the field where in former ages the blind men wandered and stumbled among the tombs. One of these ancient tombstones had been thrust across the track by some malicious person, and gave the train of cars a terrible jolt. Far up the rugged side of a mountain I perceived a rusty iron door, half overgrown with bushes and creeping plants, but with smoke issuing from its crevices.

"Is that," inquired I, "the very door in the hillside which the shepherds assured Christian was a byway to hell?"

"That was a joke on the part of the shepherds," said Mr. Smooth-it-away, with a smile. "It is neither more nor less than the door of a cavern which they use as a smoke house for the preparation of mutton hams."

My recollections of the journey are now, for a little space, dim and confused, inasmuch as a singular drowsiness here overcame me, owing to the fact that we were passing over the enchanted ground, the air of which encourages a disposition to sleep. I awoke, however, as soon as we crossed the borders of the pleasant land of Beulah. All the passengers were rubbing their eyes, comparing watches, and congratulating one another on the prospect of arriving so seasonably at the journey's end. The sweet breezes of this happy clime came refreshingly to our nostrils; we beheld the glimmering gush of silver fountains, overhung by trees of beautiful foliage and delicious fruit, which were propagated by grafts from the celestial gardens. Once, as we dashed onward like a hurricane, there was a flutter of wings and the bright appearance of an angel in the air, speeding forth on some heavenly mission. The engine now announced the close vicinity of the final station house by one last and horrible scream, in which there seemed to be distinguishable every kind of wailing and woe, and bitter fierceness of wrath, all mixed up with the wild laughter of a devil or a madman. . . .

A steam ferry boat, the last improvement on this important route, lay at the river side, puffing, snorting, and emitting all those other disagreeable utterances which betoken the departure to be immediate. I hurried on board with the rest of the passengers, most of whom were in great perturbation; some bawling out for their baggage; some tearing their hair and exclaiming that the boat would explode or sink; some already pale with the heaving of the stream; some gazing affrighted at the ugly aspect of the steersman; and some still dizzy with the slumberous influences of the Enchanted Ground. Looking back to the shore, I was amazed to discern Mr. Smooth-it-away waving his hand in token of farewell.

"Don't you go over to the Celestial City?" exclaimed I.

"O no!" answered he with a queer smile, and that same disagreeable contortion of visage which I had remarked in the inhabitants of the Dark Valley. "O no! I have come thus far only for the sake of your pleasant company. Good by! We shall meet again."

And then did my excellent friend, Mr. Smooth-it-away laugh outright, in the midst of which cachinnation a smoke-wreath issued from his mouth and nostrils, while a twinkle of lurid flame darted out of either eye, proving indubitably that his heart was all of a red blaze. The impudent fiend! To deny the existence of Tophet, when he felt its fiery tortures raging within his breast. I rushed to the side of the boat, intending to fling myself on shore; but the wheels, as they began their revolutions, threw a dash of spray over me so cold—so deadly cold, with the chill that will

never leave those waters until Death be drowned in his own
river—that, with a shiver and a heartquake I awoke. Thank
heaven it was a Dream!

8 FROM *Marvin Meyers*
The Jacksonian Persuasion

*The doubts brought on by rapid change were not limited to literary figures
or landed Federalists. Marvin Meyers in an influential book,* The
Jacksonian Persuasion *(1957), argues that the psychological tensions
generated by "the grinding uncertainties, the shocking changes, the complexity
and indirections of the new economic ways" caused the Jacksonian Democrats
to look longingly back to the simple virtues of an earlier agrarian republic.
Focusing on the Jacksonian crusade against the Second Bank of the United
States, Meyers claims that hatred of the Bank cannot be explained as the
result of economic injuries caused by that institution. Instead, he views the
Bank as a Jacksonian scapegoat; attacking it became "a way to damn the
unfamiliar" in the hope of restoring the golden age of republican simplicity.
To Meyers the stance of the Jacksonians was paradoxical in that while they
destroyed the Bank in order to restore the old order, their action actually
helped to pave the way for the triumph of laissez-faire capitalism and a new
order.*

An artful editor of the works of eminent Jacksonians might
arrange one volume to portray the revolt of the urban masses
against a business aristocracy; a second in which simple farming
folk rise against the chicanery of capitalist slickers; a third volume
tense with the struggle of the fresh forest democracy for liberation
from an effete East; and still another book of men on the make
invading the entrenched positions of chartered monopoly. With no

SOURCE. Marvin Meyers, "The Jacksonian Persuasion," *American Quarterly,* V, No.
1, (Spring, 1953), pp. 3-15. Copyright 1953, Trustees of the University of
Pennsylvania.

undue demand upon editorial resourcefulness, the Jacksonian series might turn next to the party machine, managing a newly made mass electorate through the exploitation of some of the preceding themes. The terminal volume might well rest in the shadow of Jefferson: the patriotic friends of wise and frugal government, equal rights and equal laws, strict construction and dispersed power, resisting the eternally scheming tory, monocrat, and rag-baron.

This partial list of possible uses of Jacksonian thought does not quite suggest that Jacksonian Democracy may mean all things to all men. Some omissions have been made with a point; for example, it is not suggested that any plausible editorial selection could identify Jacksonian Democracy with the rise of abolitionism; or (in an exclusive sense) with the temperance movement, school reform, religious enthusiasm or theological liberalism; or (in any sense) with Utopian community building. Yet the variety of meanings which can command some documentary support is too wide for easy assimilation in a coherent interpretation of Jacksonian Democracy. Here there is, I think, a fair field for the critical examination of the major contending theses and, of greater importance, for a fresh reading of the most obvious Jacksonian sources.

The present approach takes its departure from the debunking theses of recent writers like Dorfman and Abernethy, who in their separate ways have corrected a number of major and minor errors by an exemplary regard for original sources viewed carefully in historical context. Yet their very suspicions of such things as campaign appeals and public messages lead them to discount as meaningless a large part of the sustenance of the Jacksonian public, in order to pursue the "real thing"—i.e., the objective import of legal and institutional changes. If, for example, in Dorfman's terms, the major economic consequences of Jacksonian reform politics in New York were to establish free banking and incorporation laws and constitutional limits upon credit undertakings of the state—then what is the meaning of the highly-charged polemical jargon, the vague class appeals, the invocation of grand principles? Why, in short, did the language go so far beyond the practical object?

Simply to say "propaganda" does not tell why a particular lingo makes good propaganda and another kind does not. Nor is there obvious reason for regarding the traffic in "propaganda" as less significant intrinsically than the traffic in harder goods. And so these notes return to a staple of pre- or non-revisionist historians, the popular political discourse, in an attempt to identify the social values expressed or implied by opinion leaders of the Jacksonian persuasion.

The difficulties in such an enterprise are no doubt abundant and serious: the subject matter is in its nature elusive; the temptation is powerful indeed—as the debunking writers have been quick to note—to select passages from selected spokesmen, with considerable neglect of textual and situational context, in order to find some grand motif establishing the spirit of Jacksonian Democracy; and always one faces the relatively easy out of fabricating some systematic theory of Jacksonian Democrats from fragmentary words and acts, with results which tend to be laborious, intellectually arid,. and unrevealing of the qualities of the Jacksonian movement.

There is nevertheless a commanding case for examining the sort of values offered to and preferred by the Jacksonian public; the popular political statement would seem a prime example of such communication; and the first spokesman must be Andrew Jackson. His presidential papers taken in all their dimensions, theory, policy, and rhetoric, and searched for certain constant, elementary moral postures, provide a revealing and somewhat unexpected commentary upon the character of Jacksonian Democracy.

The Old Hero and the Restoration

Andrew Jackson, most students agree, rose to national leadership on the strength of reputed personal qualities: the blunt, tough, courageous "Old Hero" of New Orleans—honest and plain "Old Hickory." "Old" refers to age, of course, but perhaps more to "old-style." Again, not so much to old-style ideas as to the old *ways* of our fathers. He could be—and was in a boy's capacity—a fit companion for the Revolutionary heroes. Jackson never figured as the speculative statesman. In his own estimate and the public's, he was executor of a republican tradition which required not elaboration or revision but right action, taken from a firm moral stance.

It is no novelty to say that the world revealed in Andrew Jackson's public statements appears, like the public image of the man, strikingly personal and dramatic, built upon the great struggle of people *vs.* aristocracy for mastery of the republic. In relation to such issues as the Bank War, the view offers a sharp pattern: on one side, the great body of citizens, demanding only an equal chance; on the other, their temptors and adversaries, the small greedy aristocracy, full of tricks and frauds, absorbing power and privilege. Yet the grand conflict, as it emerges from Jackson's public statements, has its ambiguities—*viz.*, the variant interpretations of Jacksonian Democracy. Within the gross polemical image of social drama much remains for further explication and explanation.

On the side of virtue, in Jackson's world, one finds the plain republican—direct descendant of Jefferson's yeoman hero—along with Poor Richard and such other, lesser friends. The presence of the sturdy, independent citizen-toiler has been no secret to historians—yet some interesting possibilities have been missed. In creating the character and role of the plain republican Jackson has provided, I think, an important clue for the interpretation of Jacksonian values.

"Keep clear of Banks and indebtedness," Jackson wrote to his adopted son after settling the boy's debts," "and you live a freeman, and die in independence and leave your family so . . . and remember, my son, . . . that we should always live within our means, and not on those of others." Read this little paternal homily against the familiar public statements. Can it be that Jacksonian Democracy appeals not to some workingman's yearning for a brave new world; not to the possibilities of a fresh creation at the Western limits of civilization; not to the ambitions of a rising laissez-faire capitalism—not to any of these so much as to a *restoration* of old virtues and a (perhaps imaginary) old republican way of life?

It will be my contention that the Jacksonian appeal evokes the image of a calm and stable order of republican simplicity, content with the modest rewards of useful toil; and menacing the rustic peace, an alien spirit of risk and novelty, greed and extravagance, rapid motion and complex dealings. In short, we may discover in the political discourse of Jacksonian Democracy a powerful strain of restorationism, a stiffening of republican backs *against* the busy tinkerings, the restless projects of innovation and reform—against qualities so often set down as defining characteristics of Jacksonian America.

Of course this is not to say that the Jacksonians—master politicos and responsible rulers—designed to whisk away the given world, nor that their public actions yielded such a result. In practice they met issues as they came out of the play of current politics, adapting skillfully to the requirements of local conditions, special interests, and party rule. If the plain-republican theme is a substantial component of the Jacksonian persuasion, it need not dictate the precise policy line or control the objective consequences of party action in order to qualify as significant. The degree of coincidence or divergence is another (most important) question which cannot be approached until one knows what appeared in that dimension of political life which consists in the effective communication of value-charged language.

The Real People

Jackson's contemporary rivals damned him for appealing to class against class; some modern writers praise him for it. Beyond question, his public statements address a society divided into classes invidiously distinguished and profoundly antagonistic. But to understand the meaning of such cleavage and clash, one must see them within a controlling context. There is for Jackson a whole body, the sovereign people, beset with aristocratic sores.

The relentless and apparently irresistible use of "the people" in Jacksonian rhetoric is reflected in the diary of a wealthy New York City Whig, Philip Hone, who daily grinds the phrase through his teeth; or, with accumulated effect, in the growling humor of a Whig delegate to the New York Constitutional Convention of 1846—"The love of the people, the dear people was all that the gentlemen said influenced them. How very considerate. The love of the people—the dear people—was generally on men's tongues when they wanted to gain some particular end of their own. . . ."

In the opposition view Jackson—and Jacksonians generally—were the worst sort of demagogues who could appropriate with galling effectiveness both the dignity of the sovereign people and the passion of embattled classes. That is just the point for Jackson; nasty imputations about demagoguery aside, there are the whole people and the alien aristocracy, and the political advantages which result from the use of this distinction further confirm its validity. Jackson's notion of the-class-of-the-people is grounded first in the political order, more precisely in the republican order. From this fixed base, and with this fixed idea of the double character of the people, Jackson's representation of the group composition of society may be analyzed first in the standard terms of Jacksonian scholarship, and then, by what seems to me a necessary extension, in the context of the restoration theme.

In the most inclusive and high-toned usage, the people would comprise "all classes of the community" and "all portions of the Union." From their midst arises a general "will of the American people" which is something considerably more than a fluctuating majority vote (though the vote for Jackson is acknowledged as a fair index). There are interests of a class and sectional character, legitimate and often illegitimate; but also a pervasive common interest (which corresponds neatly with the main items of the Democratic platform). The general will is originally pure—("Never for a moment believe that the great body of the citizens of any State or States can deliberately intend to do wrong. . ."); liable to temporary error through weakness—(corruptionists will sometimes succeed in "sinister appeals to selfish feelings" and to "personal ambition"); and in the end, straight and true—("but in a community so enlightened and patriotic as the people of the United States argument will soon make them sensible of their errors").

A brief, sharp exemplification of this view occurs in Jackson's argument for direct election of the president. The extent of American territory—Madison's chief reliance for controlling the threat of majority faction—suggests to Jackson the dangerous prospect of sectional parties, which in turn will present sectional candidates and, in the zeal for party and selfish objects, "generate influences unmindful of the general good." Evil comes from the official apparatus, the mechanical contrivances of the complex electoral system. However, "the great body of the people" armed with a direct presidential vote which can express the general "will' must always defeat "antirepublican" [sic.] tendencies and secure the common good.

These "antirepublican" forces are identified as the "intriguers and politicians" and their tools, who thrive on political consolidation, chartered privilege, and speculative gain. Jackson sums up in relation to the bank war:

"The bank is, in fact, but one of the fruits of a system at war with the genius of all our institutions—a system founded upon a political creed the fundamental principle of which is a distrust of the popular will as a safe regulator of political power, and whose ultimate object and inevitable result, should it prevail, is the consolidation of all power in our system in one central government. Lavish public disbursements and corporations with exclusive privileges would be its substitutes for the original and as yet sound checks and balances of the Constitution—the means by whose silent and secret operation a control would be exercised by the few over the political conduct of the many by first acquiring that control over the labor and earnings of the great body of the people. Wherever this spirit has effected an alliance with political power, tyranny and despotism have been the fruit."

In these rough outlines there is enough to reconstruct what there is of a Jacksonian theory concerning the people and the classes. I doubt that the job is worth doing in any elaborate way. The Jacksonian persuasion is both more and much less than a theoretic structure; and Jackson's "people" are not reducible to a lump-quantity in a formal democratic scheme. What is missing is a sense of the nurture, character, and worth of the people as they are represented in Jackson's public papers. In Jackson's revealing phrase, there are still *"the real people"* to be considered.

When Jackson speaks of the people—the real people—he regularly specifies: planters and farmers, mechanics and laborers, "the bone and sinew of the country." Thus a composite class of industrious folk is marked off within society. It appears to be a narrower group than "the sovereign people" of democratic doctrine—though it would surely encompass the mass of enumerated inhabitants of the Jacksonian era. Historians who identify the favored Jacksonian class simply as the common man tell too little. Others, who make the separation upon wage-earner lines, or by rich/poor, town/country, East/West, or North/South, accept what seem to me variable secondary traits. Jackson's real people are essentially those four specified occupational groups, whose "success depends upon their own industry and economy," who know "that they must not expect to become suddenly rich by the fruits of their toil." The lines are fixed by the moral aspects of occupation.

Morals, habits, character are key terms in Jackson's discussion of the people—and almost every other subject. Major policies, for instance, are warranted by their capacity to "preserve the morals of the people," or "to revive and perpetuate those habits of economy and simplicity which are so congenial to the character of republicans." And so with the differentiation of classes according to worth: the American "laboring classes" are "so proudly distinguished" from their foreign counterparts by their "independent spirit, their love of liberty, their intelligence, and their high tone of moral character." At a still higher level within the bloc of favored classes, those who work the land—"the first and most important occupation of man"—contribute to society "that enduring wealth which is composed of flocks and herds and cultivated farms" and themselves constitute "a hardy race of free citizens."

The positive definition of the real people significantly excludes pursuits which are primarily promotional, financial, or commercial. This does not mean that Jackson raises a class war against mere occupational categories. (He was himself lawyer, office-holder, land-speculator, and merchant at various times.) The point seems to be that virtue naturally attaches to, and in fact takes much of its definition from, callings which involve some immediate engagement in the production of goods. Vice enters most readily through the excluded pursuits, though it may infect all classes and "withdraw their attention from the sober pursuits of honest industry." As indicated before, vice is to be understood largely in terms of certain occupational ways, the morals, habits, and character imputed to the trades which seek wealth without labor, employing the stratagems of speculative maneuver, privilege-grabbing, and monetary manipulation.

Like the Jeffersonians, Jackson regularly identifies the class enemy as the money power, the moneyed aristocracy, etc. There is in this undoubtedly some direct appeal against the rich. The mere words call up the income line as an immediate source of invidious distinction. Yet I would maintain that this is a secondary usage. First, Jackson's bone-and-sinew occupational classes clearly allow for a considerable income range—it would be fair to say that upper-upper and lower-lower could enter only exceptionally, while there would be a heavy concentration at the middling-independent point. Income as such does not become a ground for class preference in the usual terms of differential economic or power interest. Instead, Jackson links income with good and evil ways. The real people cannot expect sudden riches from their honest, useful work. And surplus wealth would in any case prove a temptation to the anti-republican habits of idleness and extravagance, as well as an engine of corruption. Briefly, a stable income of middling proportions is generally associated with the occupations, and with the habits, morals, and character of the real people.

More important, however, is the meaning given to phrases like "money power"—and note that Jackson typically uses this expression and not "the rich." The term occurs invariably in discussions of corporations and, particularly, of banking corporations; it signifies the *paper* money power, the *corporate* money power—i.e., concentrations of wealth arising suddenly from financial manipulation and special privilege, ill-gotten gains. If the suggestion persists in Jackson's public statements that such is the common road to wealth—and certainly the only quick way—then it is still the mode and tempo of acquisition and not the fact of possession which is made to damn the rich before Jackson's public.

Further, the money power—as I have defined it—is damned precisely as a *power,* a user of ill-gotten gains to corrupt and dominate the plain republican order. Any concentration of wealth may be a potential source of evil; but the real danger arises when the concentration falls into hands which require grants of special privilege for economic success. So a wealthy planter (and Jackson was this, too) should need no editorial or legislative hired hands; a wealthy banker cannot do without them.

Thus, Jackson's representation of the real people in the plain republican order supplies at least tentative ground for an interpretation of Jacksonian Democracy as, in vital respects, an appeal to an idealized ancestral way. Beneath the gross polemical image of people vs. aristocracy, though not at all in conflict with it, one finds the steady note of praise for simplicity and stability, self-reliance and independence, economy and useful toil, honesty and plain dealing. These ways are in themselves good, and take on the highest value when they breed a hardy race of free citizens, the plain republicans of America.

Hard Coin and the Web of Credit

As a national political phenomenon, Jacksonian Democracy drew heavily upon the Bank War for its strength and its distinctive character. The basic position Andrew Jackson established for the Democratic party in relation to money and banking continued to operate as a source of political strength through the eighteen-forties. So powerful, in fact, was the Jacksonian appeal that large sections of the rival Whig party finally capitulated on this issue explicitly for the purpose of saving the party's life. First, shrewd Whig party managers like Weed of New York, and later the generality of Whig spokesmen were forced to plead in effect: a

correct (Old Whig) position on banking is incompatible with
political survival in America.

The standard outlines of Jackson's case against banking and
currency abuses have already been sketched above. Within the
matrix of his Bank War, the crucial class split is discovered and
the general principles of Jacksonian Democracy take shape.
However, the Bank War—viewed as a struggle for possession of
men's minds and loyalties—does not simply offer a self-evident
display of its own meaning. Out of the polemical language there
emerges a basic moral posture much like the one which fixes
Jackson's representation of the republican order.

Jackson's appeal for economic reform projects, at bottom, a
dismantling operation: to pull down the menacing constructions of
federal and corporate power, and restore the wholesome rule of
"public opinion and the interests of trade." This has the sound of
laissez faire, it is laissez faire with a difference suggested by the
previous discussion of the real people and their natural, legitimate
economic interests. Poor Richard and economic man may be given
a common enemy with the plain republican; surmounting serious
difficulties, the forest democrat, poor man, and workingman might
be recruited for the same cause. Indeed the sweeping effect of
Jackson's negative case may be explained in part by his touching
off a common hatred of an all-purpose villain. Yet, if the dismantling operation gives promise of catching several particular
enemies in the broad aristocracy trap, does it not promise still
more winningly a dismantling, and a restoration of pure and
simple ways?

Tocqueville, though he reaches an opposite conclusion, suggests
very effectively this unmaking spirit:

"The bank is a great establishment, which has an independent
existence; and the people, accustomed to make and unmake
whatsoever they please, are startled to meet with this obstacle to
their authority. In the midst of the perpetual fluctuation of
society, the community is irritated by so permanent an institution
and is led to attack it, in order to see whether it can be shaken,
like everything else."

But what is it about the great establishment which provokes
hostility and a passion for dismantling? How can the permanence
of the Bank, set over against the perpetual fluctuation of society,
explain the ceaseless Jacksonian complaint against the tendency of
the Bank to introduce perpetual fluctuation in the economic affairs

of society? There is, I think, another and better explanation of the symbolic import of the Bank War.

The Bank of the United States, veritable incarnation of evil in Jackson's argument, assumes the shape of "the monster," which is to say, the unnatural creature of greed for wealth and power. Its managers, supporters, and beneficiaries form the first rank of the aristocracy, i.e., the artificial product of legislative prestidigitation. The monster thrives in a medium of paper money, the mere specter of palpable value. The bank system suspends the real world of solid goods, honestly exchanged, upon a mysterious, swaying web of speculative credit. The natural distributive mechanism, which proportions rewards to "industry, economy, and virtue," is fixed to pay off the insider and the gambler.

To knock down this institution, then, and with it a false, rotten, insubstantial world, becomes the compelling object of Jackson's case. He removed the public deposits, so he said, "to preserve the morals of the people, the freedom of the press, and the purity of the elective franchise." Final victory over the Bank and its paper spawn "will form an era in the history of our country which will be dwelt upon with delight by every true friend of its liberty and independence," not least because the dismantling operation will "do more to revive and perpetuate those habits of economy and simplicity which are so congenial to the character of republicans than all the legislation which has yet been attempted."

The Jacksonian appeal for a dismantling operation and the restoration of old republican ways flows easily into the course of the hard coin argument. Hard coin, I have already suggested, stands for palpable value as against the spectral issue of the printing press. In plainer terms, Jackson argues before the Congress: "The great desideratum in modern times is an efficient check upon the power of banks, preventing that excessive issue of paper whence arise those fluctuations in the standard of value which render uncertain the rewards of labor." Addressing a later Congress, Jackson pursues the point: Bank paper lacks the stability provided by hard coin; thus circulation varies with the tide of bank issue; thus the value of property and the whole price level are at the mercy of these banking institutions; thus the laboring classes especially, and the real people generally, are victimized, while the few conniving speculators add to their riches.

A related appeal to the attractions of stability, of sure rewards and steady values and hard coins, can be found in Jackson's warnings against the accumulation and distribution of the revenue surplus: an overflowing federal treasury, spilling into the states, would produce ruinous expansions and contractions of credit, arbitrary fluctuations in the price of property, "rash speculation, idleness, extravagance, and a deterioration of morals." But above all it is the banks and their paper system which "engender a spirit of speculation injurious to the habits and character of the people," which inspire "this eager desire to amass wealth without labor," which turn even good men from "the sober pursuits of honest industry." To restore hard coin is to restore the ways of the plain republican order. Dismantling of the unnatural and unjust bank and paper system is the necessary first step.

The Sum of Good Government

The one essential credential of public or private worth—whether of individual, or class, or trade—is conveyed by Jackson through the term "republican"; that which is anti-republican is the heart of evil. With all valuations refered to the republican standard, and that standard apparently a category of politics, one might expect some final revelation of the Jacksonian persuasion in Jackson's representation of the good state. The truth is, on my reading, somewhat different: Jackson rather defines republican by ways of living and working, than refers those ways to republicanism in the strict political sense. The good republic he projects—and remembers from the Revolutionary days of '76 and 1800—is on the political side the ornament, the glory, and the final security of the worthy community, not its creator.

Jackson's sketch of a political system congenial to old republican ways uses nothing beyond the memorable summation in Jefferson's First Inaugural Address: "a wise and frugal government, which shall restrain men from injuring one another, shall leave them otherwise free to regulate their own pursuits of industry and improvement, and shall not take from the mouth of labor the bread it has earned. This is the sum of good government, and this is necessary to close the circle of our felicities." The literal Jacksonian translation prescribes: the Constitution strictly construed; strict observance of the 'fundamental and sacred" rules of simplicity and economy; separation of the political power from the conduct of economic affairs.

His political appeal both parallels and supports the general themes discussed in previous sections. This is no government of

projects and ambitions. It does its simple, largely negative business
in a simple, self-denying way. Firm and strong, it trims drastically
the apparatus of power. The hardy race of independent
republicans, engaged in plain and useful toil, require no more than
a stable government of equal laws to secure them in their equal
rights. In Jacksonian discourse, government becomes a fighting
issue only when it grows too fat and meddlesome. Again, the
republic is defined and judged positively by its republicans and
only negatively by its government.

The Bank War once more provides the crucial case. Jackson
mobilized the powers of government for what was essentially a
dismantling operation. His cure avoids with terror any transfer-
ence of the powers of the Bank to another agency: to give to the
president the currency controls and the power over individuals
now held by the Bank "would be as objectionable and as dangerous as to leave it as it is." Control of banks and currency—apart
from the strictly constitutional functions of coinage and regulation
of value—should be "entirely separated from the political power of
the country." Any device is wicked and dangerous which would
"concentrate the whole moneyed power of the Republic in any
form whatsoever." We must, above all, ignore petty, expediential
considerations, and "look to the honor and preservation of the
republican system."

Paradox

And so the circuit of Jackson's public appeal may be closed.
Plain, honest men; simple, stable economy; wise and frugal
government. It reads less as the herald of modern times and a
grand project of reform than as a reaction against the spirit and
body of the changing world. Jacksonian Democracy, viewed
through Jackson's public statements, wants to undo far more than
it wishes to do; and not for the purpose of a fresh creation, but for
the restoration of an old republican idyl. The tremendous popularity of Andrew Jackson and his undoubted public influence
sugggest that this theme can be ignored only at great peril in any
general interpretation of Jacksonian Democracy. We must prepare
for a paradox: the movement which in many ways cleared the
path for the triumph of laissez-faire capitalism and its culture in
America, and the public which in its daily life acted out that
victory, held nevertheless in their conscience an image of a chaste

republican order, resisting the seductions of risk and novelty, greed and extravagance, rapid motion and complex dealings.

9 FROM   *Editors of The American Review*
Influence of the Trading Spirit Upon the Social and Moral Life of America

Marvin Meyers' explanation of "the Jacksonian persuasion" (selection 8) sheds much light on the period. However, it could be argued that Whigs as well as Jacksonians often despaired over the passing of the seemingly golden age of stable, agrarian republicanism. Furthermore, as this article published in a leading Whig journal attests, the expressions of nostalgia for the simpler virtues of the idealized Jeffersonian yeoman were not merely expedient political statements.

The American Review *was founded in 1845 by George Hooker Colton and the nation's leading Whigs to counter the influence of the Jacksonian journal,* The Democratic Review. *Generally speaking,* The American Review *praised the Whig principles of economic progress through government encouragement. Yet on many occasions, doubts about the nature of America's economic advance were clearly expressed by these same champions of industrial enterprise. This article suggests that the chief results of the restless pursuit of wealth were anxieties, unhappiness, and a loss of human kindness.*

Those influences which affect the characters of a whole people are less observed, although more important, than such as are peculiar to classes or individuals. The exertions which one may make to protect himself from error, or demeaning influences, are sometimes rendered ineffectual from his ignorance of the tremendous biases which he receives from a corrupt public opinion; as

SOURCE. *The American Review: A Whig Journal of Politics, Literature, Art and Science,* I (January 1845), pp. 95-98.

the most careful observations of the mariner are sometimes vitiated by an unknown current which insensibly drifts him from his supposed position. What everybody does in our own community, we are apt to suppose to be universal with men; and universal custom is, by general consent, not to be disputed. We are not disposed to suspect public opinion, or to question common custom.—Nay, we do not even, for the most part, distinguish between a prevailing sentiment and an innate idea—between a universal or national habit and a law of nature. The customs of the city in which we are brought up seem to most persons of divine appointment. We are apt to account a foreigner who prefers (in accordance with his own national manners and prejudices) a different division of the day, different hours at the table, a different style of dress, as almost immoral. This proves how little aware we may be of the nature of the social habits and sentiments which greatly influence our characters. We propose to offer a few observations upon some of our national habits and tendencies. . . .

All strangers who come among us remark the excessive anxiety written in the American countenance. The widespread comfort, the facilities for livelihood, the spontaneous and cheap lands, the high price of labor, are equally observed, and render it difficult to account for these lines of painful thoughtfulness. It is not poverty, nor tyranny, nor over-competition which produces this anxiety; that is clear. It is the concentration of the faculties upon an object, which in its very nature is unattainable—the perpetual improvement of the outward condition. There are no bounds among us to the restless desire to be better off; and this is the ambition of all classes of society. We are not prepared to allow that wealth is more valued in America than elsewhere, but in other countries the successful pursuit of it is necessarily confined to a few, while here it is open to all. No man in America is contented to be poor, or expects to continue so. There are here no established limits within which the hopes of any class of society must be confined, as in other countries. There is consequently no condition of hopes realized, in other words, of contentment. In other lands, if children can maintain the station and enjoy the means, however moderate, of their father, they are happy. Not so with us. This is not the spirit of our institutions. Nor will it long be otherwise in other countries. That equality, that breaking down of artificial barriers which has produced this universal ambition and restless activity in America, is destined to prevail throughout the earth. But because we are in advance of the world in the great political principle, and are now experiencing some of its first effects, let us not mistake these for the desirable fruits of freedom. Commerce is to become the universal pursuit of men. It is to be the first result of freedom, of popular institutions everywhere. Indeed, every land not steeped in tyranny is now feeling this impulse. But while trade is destined to free and employ the masses, it is also destined to destroy for the time much of the beauty and happiness of every land. This has been the result in our own country. We are free. It is a glorious thing that we have no serfs, with the large and unfortunate exception of our slaves—no artificial distinctions—no acknowledged superiority of blood—no station which merit may not fill—no rounds in the social ladder to which the humblest may not aspire. But the excitement, the commercial activity, the restlessness, to which this state of things has given birth, is far from being a desirable or a natural condition. It is natural to the circumstances, but not natural to the human soul. It is good and hopeful to the interests of the race, but destructive to the happiness, and dangerous to the virtue of the generation exposed to it.

Those unaccustomed, by reading or travel, to other states of society, are probably not aware how very peculiar our manner of life here is. The laboriousness of Americans is beyond all comparison, should we except the starving operatives of English factories. And when we consider that here, to the labor of the body is added the great additional labor of mental responsibility and ambition, it is not to be wondered at that as a race, the commercial population is dwindling in size, and emaciated in health, so that *palor* is the national complexion. If this devotion to business were indispensable to living, it would demand our pity. It is unavoidable, we know, in one sense. That is, it is customary—it is universal. There is no necessity for the custom; but there is a necessity, weakly constituted as men are, that every individual should conform greatly to the prevailing habits of his fellows, and the expectations of the community in and with which he deals. It is thus that those who deeply feel the essentially demoralizing and wretched influences of this system are yet doomed to be victims of it. Nay, we are all, no matter what our occupations, more or less, and all greatly, sufferers from the excessive stimulus under which every thing is done. We are all worn out with thought that does not develop our thinking faculties in a right direction, and with feeling expended upon poor and low objects. There is no profession that does not feel it. The lawyer must confine himself to his office, without vacation, to adjust a business which never sleeps or relaxes. The physician must labor day and night to repair bodies, never well from over-exertion, over-excitement, and over-indulgence. The minister must stimulate himself to supply the cravings of diseased moral appetites, and to arouse the attention of men deafened by the noise, and dizzy with the whirl in which they constantly live.

We call our country a *happy* country; happy, indeed, in being the home of noble political institutions, the abode of freedom; but very far from being happy in possessing a cheerful, light-hearted, and joyous people. Our agricultural regions even are infected with the same anxious spirit of gain. If ever the curse of labor was upon the race, it is upon us; nor is it simply now "by the sweat of thy brow thou shalt earn thy bread." Labor for a livelihood is dignified. But we labor for bread, and labor for pride, and *labor* for pleasure. A man's life with us *does* consist of the abundance of the things which he possesseth. To get, and to have the reputation of possessing, is the ruling passion. To it are bent all the energies of nine-tenths of our population. Is it that our people are so much more miserly and earth-born than any other? No, not by any constitutional baseness; but circumstances have necessarily given this direction to the American mind. In the hard soil of our common mother, New England—the poverty of our ancestors—their early thrift and industry—the want of other distinctions than those of property—the frown of the Puritans upon all pleasures; these circumstances combined, directed our energies from the first into the single channel of trade. And in that they have run till they have gained a tremendous head, and threaten to convert our whole people into mere money-changers and producers. Honor belongs to our fathers, who in times of great necessity met the demand for a most painful industry with such manly and unflinching hearts. But what was their hard necessity we are perpetuating as our willing servitude! what they bore as evil we seek as good. We cannot say that the destiny of this country did not demand that the spirit of trade should rule it for centuries. It may be that we are now carrying out only the decree of Providence. But if so, let us consider ourselves as in the wilderness, and not in the promised land. Let us bear the dispensation of God, but not glory in our bondage. If we are doomed to be tradesmen, and nothing but tradesmen—if money, and its influences and authority, are to reign for a season over our whole land, let us not mistake it for the kingdom of heaven, and build triumphal arches over our

avenues of trade, as though the Prince of Peace and the Son of
God were now and thus to enter in.

It is said that we are not a happy people. And it is true; for we
most unwisely neglect all those free fountains of happiness which
Providence has opened for all its children. Blessed beyond any
people with the means of living, supplied to an unparalleled extent
with the comforts and luxuries of life, our American homes are
sombre and cheerless abodes. There is even in the air of comfort
which their well-furnished apartments wear something uncomfor-
table. They are the habitations of those who do not live at home.
They are wanting in a social and cheerful aspect. They seem fitted
more to be admired than to be enjoyed. The best part of the house
is for the occasional use of strangers, and not to be occupied by
those who might, day by day, enjoy it, which is but one proof
among many that we love to appear comfortable rather than to be
so. Thus miserable pride hangs like a mill stone about our
hospitality. "We sacrifice the hospitality of a year to the prodigal-
ity of a night." We are ashamed of any thing but affluence, and
when we cannot make an appearance, or furnish entertainments as
showy as the richest, we will do nothing. Thus does pride close our
doors. Hospitality becomes an event of importance. It is not our
daily life, one of our chiefest enjoyments, but a debt, a ceremony, a
penance. And not only pride, but anxiety of mind, interferes with
sociality. Bent upon one aim, the merchant grudges his thoughts.
He cannot expend his energies in social enjoyment. Nay, it is not
enjoyment to him; society has nothing of the excitement of
business. The excessive pursuit of gain begets a secrecy of thought,
a contradiction of ideas, a barrenness of interest, which renders its
votary any thing but social or companionable. Conversation
incessantly takes an anxious and uninteresting turn; and the
fireside becomes only a narrower exchange, and the parlor a more
private news-room.

It is rare to see a foreigner without some taste for amusement,
some power of relaxing his mind, some interest in the arts, or in
literature. This is true even of the less privileged classes. It is rare,
on the contrary, to find a virtuous American past middle life, who
does not regard amusements of all sorts either as childish or
immoral; who possesses any acquaintance with or taste for the
arts, except it be a natural and rude taste for music; or who reads
any thing except newspapers, and only the political or commercial
columns of those. It is the want of tastes for other things than
business which gives an anxious and unhappy turn to our minds.

It cannot be many years before the madness of devoting the whole day to the toils of the countinghouse will be acknowledged; before the claim of body and mind to relaxation and cheerful, exhilarating amusement will be seen. We consider the common suspicion which is felt of amusements among thoughtful people to be one of the most serious evils to which our community is exposed. It outlaws a natural taste, and violates and ruins the consciences of the young, by stamping as sinful what they have not the force to refrain from. It makes our places of amusement low, divides the thoughtful and the careless, the grave and the gay, the old and the young, in their pleasures. Children are without the protection of their parents in their enjoyments. And thus, too, is originated one of the greatest curses of our social state—the great want of intimacy and confidence between children and their parents, especially between fathers and sons. . . .

While the commercial spirit in this extravagant form gives a certain sobriety and moral aspect to society, it occasions an excessive barrenness of real moral excellencies. This is a very difficult and delicate distinction to render popularly apparent, although of the most vital and substantial reality. There is a very great difference between what are called strict morals, and morals that are really profound in their sources, and pervading in their influence. We are more strict in our morals in these Northern States than anywhere in the world, but it is questionable whether our morality is not of a somewhat inferior quality, and in a too narrow view. It is artificial, conventional. There is no quarter of the earth where the Sabbath is more scrupulously observed—where religious institutions are so well supported, or where more abstinence from pleasure is practised. The great virtue of industry prevails. Overt sins are more rare here than elsewhere. As far as morality is restrictive in its nature, it has accomplished a great work in America. The vices or sins which are reducible to statute, or known by name, are generally restrained. We have a large class of persons of extraordinary propriety and faultlessness of life. Our view of morals has a tendency to increase this class. Our pursuits are favorable to it. The love of gain is one of the most sober of all desires. . . . Our moral sense operates only in one direction. Our virtues are the virtues of merchants, and not of men. We run all to honesty, and mercantile honesty. We do not cultivate the graces of humanity. We have more conscience than heart, and more propriety than either. The fear of evil consequences is more influential than the love of goodness. There is nothing hearty, gushing, eloquent, in the national virtue. You do not see goodness leaking out from the full vessel at every motion it feels. Our goodness is formal, deliberate, premeditated. The upright man is not benevolent, and the just man is not generous. The good man is not cheerful. The religious man is not agreeable. In other words, our morals are partial, and therefore barren. . . .For our part, we are ready to say, let us have more faults and more virtues; more weaknesses and more graces; less punctilio, and more affluence of heart. Let us be less dignified and more cordial; less sanctimonious and more unselfish; less thriving and more cheerful; less toilsome and more social. . . .

10 FROM

Eliza Cooke and Henry Russel
The Old Arm Chair

One of the best indicators of social values, although it is frequently overlooked by historians, is the popular music of an age. In bustling Jacksonian America, an era of factories and railroads, popular songs were invariably sentimental, nostalgic, and antimaterialistic, reflecting again the ambiguous attitude most Americans had concerning their future. Best-selling songs like John Howard Payne's "Home Sweet Home" (1823), Samuel Woodworth's "The Old Oaken Bucket" (1825), and George P. Morris' "Woodman, Spare That Tree" (1837) evoked a simple rural past in which reverence for family, home, and nature were celebrated in a wistful and melancholy manner.

"The Old Arm Chair" is an excellent example of the type of music sung and listened to in the Middle Period. Written by Eliza Cooke with music by the popular British baritone, Henry Russell, "The Old Arm Chair" was America's most popular song in 1840, outselling even the political favorite "Tippecanoe and Tyler Too." As "The Old Arm Chair" suggests, motherhood was central to the popular culture of the age. In the increasingly achievement-oriented and materialistic society, women, and especially mothers, were idealized as moral, redemptive forces, preserving the sanctity of the home. The mother cult found expression in much of the literature of the period, including the widely read poetry of Longfellow, Lowell, and Whittier.

SOURCE. *The Treasury of Song for the Home Circle.* . . (Philadelphia, Hubbard Brothers, Publishers, 1882), pp. 174-177.

THE OLD ARM CHAIR.

I love it, I love it, and who shall dare To chide me for loving that old arm chair; I've treasured it long as a ho - ly prize, I've be - dew'd it with tears, and embalm'd it with sighs; 'Tis bound by a thou - sand bands to my heart, Not a tie will break, not a

THE OLD ARM CHAIR.

link will start. Would ye learn the spell, a mother sat there, And a

sa - cred thing is that old arm chair.

I sat and watch'd her ma - ny a day, When her eye grew dim, and her

locks were grey, And I almost worship'd her when she smil'd, And turn'd from her Bible to

bless her child. Years roll'd on, but the last one sped, My i-dol was shatter'd, my

earth-star fled; I learnt how much the heart can bear, When I saw her die in that

old arm chair.   'Tis past! 'tis past! but I

gaze on it now With quivering breath, and throbbing brow, 'Twas there she nurs'd me, 'twas

there she died; And mem - 'ry flows with la - va tide.

Say it is fol - ly, and deem me weak, While the scald - ing drops start

down my cheek; But I love it, I love it, and can - not tear My

soul from a mother's old arm chair.

11 FROM *Alexis de Tocqueville*
Causes of the Restless Spirit of the Americans in the Midst of Their Prosperity

According to Alexis de Tocqueville, the most brilliant of the many foreign observers of Jacksonian America, the greatest cause of consternation in this country was that equal opportunity had "opened the door to universal competition." All men thought in terms of bettering themselves, and this accounted both for the great physical and material mobility and the "strange unrest" that Tocqueville noted. This helps explain the paradox of how an optimistic people, believing in progress and a providential destiny, could also be, as an 1836 traveler stated, "an anxious, care-worn people." "In no country are the faces of the people furrowed with harder lines of care," wrote a disillusioned American doctor, Thomas Low Nichols. "In no country that I know of is there so much hard, toilsome, unremitting labour; in none so little of recreation and enjoyment of life. Work and worry eat out the hearts of the people, and they die before their time. It is a hard story, but it is a true one."

In certain remote corners of the Old World you may still sometimes stumble upon a small district which seems to have been forgotten amidst the general tumult, and to have remained stationary whilst everything around it was in motion. The inhabitants are for the most part extremely ignorant and poor; they take no part in the business of the country, and they are frequently oppressed by the government; yet their countenances are generally placid, and their spirits light. In America I saw the freest and most enlightened men, placed in the happiest circumstances which the world affords: it seemed to me as if a cloud habitually hung upon their brow, and I thought them serious and almost sad even in their pleasures. The chief reason of this contrast is that the former do not think of the ills they endure—the latter are forever brooding over advantages they do not possess. It is strange to see with what

SOURCE. Alexis de Tocqueville, *Democracy in America,* trans. Henry Reeve (2 vols., London, New York, The Colonial Press, 1900), II, pp. 144-147.

feverish ardor the Americans pursue their own welfare; and to watch the vague dread that constantly torments them lest they should not have chosen the shortest path which may lead to it. A native of the United States clings to this world's goods as if he were certain never to die; and he is so hasty in grasping at all within his reach, that one would suppose he was constantly afraid of not living long enough to enjoy them. He clutches everything, he holds nothing fast, but soon loosens his grasp to pursue fresh gratifications.

In the United States a man builds a house to spend his latter years in it, and he sells it before the roof is on: he plants a garden, and lets it just as the trees are coming into bearing: he brings a field into tillage, and leaves other men to gather the crops: he embraces a profession, and gives it up: he settles in a place, which he soon afterwards leaves, to carry his changeable longings elsewhere. If his private affairs leave him any leisure, he instantly plunges into the vortex of politics; and if at the end of a year of unremitting labor he finds he has a few days' vacation, his eager curiosity whirls him over the vast extent of the United States, and he will travel fifteen hundred miles in a few days, to shake off his happiness. Death at length overtakes him, but it is before he is weary of his bootless chase of that complete felicity which is forever on the wing.

At first sight there is something surprising in this strange unrest of so many happy men, restless in the midst of abundance. The spectacle itself is however as old as the world; the novelty is to see a whole people furnish an exemplification of it. Their taste for physical gratifications must be regarded as the original source of that secret inquietude which the actions of the Americans betray, and of that inconstancy of which they afford fresh examples every day. He who has set his heart exclusively upon the pursuit of worldly welfare is always in a hurry, for he has but a limited time at his disposal to reach it, to grasp it, and to enjoy it. The recollection of the brevity of life is a constant spur to him. Besides the good things which he possesses, he every instant fancies a thousand others which death will prevent him from trying if he does not try them soon. This thought fills him with anxiety, fear, and regret, and keeps his mind in ceaseless trepidation, which leads him perpetually to change his plans and his abode. If in addition to the taste for physical well-being a social condition be superadded, in which the laws and customs make no condition permanent, here is a great additional stimulant to this restlessness of temper. Men will then be seen continually to change their track, for fear of missing the shortest cut to happiness. It may readily be conceived that if men, passionately bent upon physical gratifications, desire eagerly, they are also easily discouraged: as their ultimate object is to enjoy, the means to reach that object must be prompt and easy, or the trouble of acquiring the gratification would be greater than the gratification itself. Their prevailing frame of mind then is at once ardent and relaxed, violent and enervated. Death is often less dreaded than perseverance in continuous efforts to one end.

The equality of conditions leads by a still straighter road to several of the effects which I have here described. When all the privileges of birth and fortune are abolished, when all professions are accessible to all, and a man's own energies may place him at the top of any one of them, an easy and unbounded career seems open to his ambition, and he will readily persuade himself that he is born to no vulgar destinies. But this is an erroneous notion, which is corrected by daily experience. The same equality which allows every citizen to conceive these lofty hopes, renders all the citizens less able to realize them: it circumscribes their powers on every side, whilst it gives freer scope to their desires. Not only are they themselves powerless, but they are met at every step by immense obstacles, which they did not at first perceive. They have swept away the privileges of some of their fellow-creatures which stood in their way, but they have opened the door to universal competition: the barrier has changed its shape rather than its position. When men are nearly alike, and all follow the same track, it is very difficult for any one individual to walk quick and cleave a way through the dense throng which surrounds and presses him. This constant strife between the propensities springing from the equality of conditions and the means it supplies to satisfy them, harasses and wearies the mind.

It is possible to conceive men arrived at a degree of freedom which should completely content them; they would then enjoy their independence without anxiety and without impatience. But men will never establish any equality with which they can be contented. Whatever efforts a people may make, they will never succeed in reducing all the conditions of society to a perfect level; and even if they unhappily attained that absolute and complete depression, the inequality of minds would still remain, which, coming directly from the hand of God, will forever escape the laws of man. However democratic then the social state and the political constitution of a people may be, it is certain that every member of the community will always find out several points about him which command his own position; and we may foresee that his looks will be doggedly fixed in that direction. When inequality of conditions is the common law of society, the most marked inequalities do not strike the eye: when everything is nearly on the same level, the slightest are marked enough to hurt it. Hence the desire of equality always becomes more insatiable in proportion as equality is more complete.

Amongst democratic nations men easily attain a certain equality of conditions: they can never attain the equality they desire. It perpetually retires from before them, yet without hiding itself from their sight, and in retiring draws them on. At every moment they think they are about to grasp it; it escapes at every moment from their hold. They are near enough to see its charms, but too far off to enjoy them; and before they have fully tasted its delights they die. To these causes must be attributed that strange melancholy which oftentimes will haunt the inhabitants of democratic countries in the midst of their abundance, and that disgust at life which sometimes seizes upon them in the midst of calm and easy circumstances. Complaints are made in France that the number of suicides increases; in America suicide is rare, but insanity is said to be more common than anywhere else. These are all different symptoms of the same disease. The Americans do not put an end to their lives, however disquieted they may be, because their religion forbids it; and amongst them materialism may be said hardly to exist, notwithstanding the general passion for physical gratification. The will resists—reason frequently gives way.

In democratic ages enjoyments are more intense than in the ages of aristocracy, and especially the number of those who partake in them is larger: but, on the other hand, it must be admitted that man's hopes and his desires are oftener blasted, the soul is more stricken and perturbed, and care itself more keen.

12 FROM Michael Chevalier
Symptoms of Revolution

On a cruder level the anxieties and frustrations of the period often vented themselves in acts of violence. Riots, street fights, duels, lynchings, and incendiarism were endemic to Jacksonian America.

Michael Chevalier, reflecting on the violence in America of the 1830's, found that "unfortunately, reverence for the laws seems to be disappearing among Americans." In the very preceptive selection that follows, entitled "Symptoms of Revolution," Chevalier views the increased violence as a failure of the political order to keep pace with the rapid process of economic and social change. "The present generation in the United States," he wrote, "brought up in devotion to business, living in an atmosphere of self-interest, if it is superior to the last generation in commercial intelligence and industrial enterprise, is inferior to it in civil courage and love of public good." The American political system, he concluded, "no longer works well. . . .Everywhere, the relations established by the old federal compact are unfitted to the new state of things."

LETTER XXX. SYMPTOMS OF REVOLUTION.

BALTIMORE, SEPTEMBER 25, 1835

Two years ago Mr. Clay began a speech in the Senate, with these words, which have become celebrated on this side of the Atlantic: "We are in the midst of a revolution." It was at the time, when by an act of authority before unheard of in American history, General Jackson had just settled the bank question, which his friends in Congress and even his own ministers had refused to decide. These words have often been repeated by others. More recently, since the scenes of murder, outrage, and destruction

SOURCE. Michael Chevalier, *Society, Manners and Politics in the United States: Being a Series of Letters on North America* (Boston, Weeks, Jordan and Company, 1839), pp. 385-395.

which have been exhibited through the United States, both in the slave-holding States, and in those in which slavery does not exist, in the country as well as in the towns, at Boston, the republican city *par excellence,* as well as at Baltimore, for which the bloody excesses of which it was the theatre in 1812, have gained the title of the *Mob Town,* good citizens have repeated with grief; "We are in the midst of a revolution . . ."

Unfortunately the reverence for the laws seems to be wearing out with the Americans. This people, eminently practical in every thing else, have allowed themselves to be pushed into the excess of theory in politics, and have here taken up the *quand meme* logic; they have shrunk from none of the consequences of popular sovereignty, at least while those consequences were flattering to their pride; as if there were a single principle in the world, not excepting Christian charity itself, which could be carried to its extreme logical consequences without resulting in absolute absurdity. They have, therefore, been driven in the United States to deny that there is any principle true in and by itself, and to assert that the will of the people is, always and necessarily, justice; the infallibility of the people in every thing and at all times, has, in fact, become the received doctrine, and thus a door has been opened to the tyranny of a turbulent minority, which always calls itself the people.

The appearance of this miscalled popular justice, administered by the hands of a few desperate or furious men, who call themselves the successors of the Boston *Tea Party* of 1773, is a great calamity in the bosom of a country, where there is no other guarantee of the public peace than a reverence of the laws, and where the legislator, taking for granted the prevalence of order, has made no provisions against disorder. This popular justice has the greater condemnation of being for the most part grossly unjust. Most of the men who have been atrociously hanged, or flogged, or tortured in twenty other ways in the South, as abolitionists, that is as guilty of instigating the slaves to rise against their masters, were, according to all appearances, merely guilty of having expressed their abhorrence of slavery with too little caution. It is even doubtful whether the pretended plots, for being engaged in which whites and blacks have been summarily executed, had a real existence. At least no proof of their reality has yet been brought forward, which would be admitted by a court of justice.

During the outrages last month at Baltimore, which were continued for four days, this self-styled justice was most stupidly
unjust. . . .

These disorders are alarming from their general prevalence, and
from their frequent repetitions, and they are the more so, the less
their importance is realised. They meet with few voices to con-
demn them, but they find many to excuse them. One of the defects
of democracy is that it is forgetful of the past, and careless of the
future. A riot, which in France would put a stop to business,
prevents no one here from going to the Exchange, speculating,
turning over the dollars, and making money. On meeting in the
morning, each one asks and tells us the news; here a negro has
been hanged, there a white man has been flogged; at Philadelphia,
ten houses have been demolished; at Buffalo, at Utica, some people
of colour have been scourged. Then they go on to the price of
cotton and coffee, the arrivals of flour, lumber, and tobacco, and
become absorbed in calculations the rest of the day. I am surprised
to see how dead the word equality falls, when a good citizen
pronounces it; the reign of law seems to be at an end; we have
fallen under that of expediency. Farewell to justice, farewell to the
great principles of 1776 and 1789! All hail to the interest of the
moment, interpreted by nobody knows who, for the success of some
petty intrigue of politics or business!. . .

It would seem as if political principles no longer existed in the
United States but at the pleasure of the passions, and the laws had
no force when they jarred with interest. When a State feels itself
injured by a tariff, it declares the law null and void, arms its
militia, buys powder and throws down the glove to Congress.
When another State, as Ohio, is dissatisfied with the boundary
line assigned to it, it declares war against Michigan, its neighbour,
in order to extend its frontiers by force. When the fanatics of
Massachusetts, in their savage intolerance, feel offended by the
presence of a Catholic convent, in which the sisters devote
themselves to the work of educating young girls without distinction of sect, they plunder it and set it on fire, and the sacred
edifice is burnt, in sight of a city with 70,000 inhabitants, without
a drop of water being thrown upon the flames, and without its
being possible to find a jury that would convict the authors of the
cowardly outrage. When a Governor of Georgia comes into
collision with an upright magistrate, who interposes his authority
between the rapacity of the whites and the poor Indian whom they

are impatient to rob, he denounces the just judge to the legislature, and urges the passing of a law that will make him a State criminal. And, I repeat it, the worst and most fatal symptom of the times is, that the perpetration of these outrages, however frequent they become, excites no sensation. The destruction of the churches and school-houses of the blacks in New York was looked upon as a show, and the merchants of the city as they passed, paused to take a moment's relaxation from the sight; the fall of the buildings was greeted with loud cheers. In Baltimore, a numerous crowd applauded the work of demolition without inquiring whose house was pulled down, and the women, in the excitement of the moment, waved their handkerchiefs in the air. . . .

The present generation in the United States, brought up in devotion to business, living in an atmosphere of interest, if it is superiour to the last generation in commercial intelligence and industrial enterprise, is inferiour to it in civil courage and love of the public good. . . .

The American system no longer works well. In the North, the removal of all restrictions on the right of suffrage, without the creation of any counterpoise, has destroyed the equilibrium. In the South, the old foundation borrowed from the ante-Christian ages, on which it has been attempted to raise the superstructure of a new social order in the nineteenth century, shakes and threatens to bury the thoughtless builders under the ruins of their half-finished work. In the West, a population sprung from the soil under the influence of circumstances unparallelled in the history of the world, already affects a superiority, or rather lays claim to dominion, over the North and South. Everywhere, the relations established by the old federal compact, become unsuited to the new state of things. The dissolution of the Union, the mere thought of which would have caused a shudder of horrour, ten years ago, which was numbered among those acts of infamy that are not to be named,—the dissolution of the Union has been demanded, and no thunder fell upon the head of the perpetrator of the sacrilege. At present it is a common topic of conversation. The dissolution of the Union, if it should take place, would be the most complete of all revolutions.

What will be the character of this revolution, which is felt to be approaching? To what institutions will it give birth? Who must perish in the day of account? Who will rise on the storm? Who will resist the action of ages? I have not the gift of prophecy, and I shall not try to pierce the mystery of the destinies of the New

World. But I have a firm faith, that a people with the energy and intelligence which the Americans possess; a people which has like it the genius of industry, which combines perseverance with the resources of ingenuity, which is essentially regular in its habits and orderly in its disposition,which is deeply imbued with religious habits, even when a lively faith is wanting, such a people cannot be born of yesterday to vanish on the morrow. The American people, in spite of its original defects, in spite of the numerous voids which a hasty growth and a superficial education have left in its ideas, feelings, and customs, is still a great and powerful people. For such nations, the most violent storms are wholesome trials which strengthen, solemn warnings which teach, elevate, and purify them.

PART THREE
Politics and Reform

13 FROM Richard Hofstadter
Toward a Party System

It would be pleasant to relate that the various crises and tensions of the period were suddenly resolved by the triumphant appearance on the political scene of Andrew Jackson—uniting West with East, spreading democracy everywhere. This, however, was not the case. Two-party politics as it reemerged in the Jacksonian era was characterized by coalition parties seeking to win the support of the broadest possible electorate. These parties tended to be conservative and nonideological. Basic economic, social, and moral issues were either ignored or compromised; they were seldom dealt with in an effective manner.

The new politics that emerged in the 1820's came to be dominated by specialists—not the statesman, lawyer, merchant, or planter of an earlier era. Men like Madison, Monroe, and John Quincy Adams—high-minded persons with broad visions—gradually gave way to the professional politicians, the Thurlow Weeds, Amos Kendalls, and Martin Van Burens—individuals more

SOURCE. Richard Hofstadter, *The Idea of a Party System: The Rise of Legitimate Opposition in the United States, 1780-1840* (Berkeley and Los Angeles, 1969), pp. 212-214, 217, 223-226. Originally published by the University of California Press, reprinted by permission of the Regents of the University of California.

concerned with party success than with the implementation of principles.
These men depended for their success on highly disciplined party orga-
nizations that could gain wide popular support.

The concept of party itself was changing in the twenties. The traditional
view of political parties, inherited from British and colonial experience, was a
negative one. They were regarded as dangerous factions based on family,
friendship, and special interest. Yet during the 1820's in states such as New
York, Pennsylvania, New Jersey, Massachusetts, and North Carolina,
younger professional politicians developed the modern view of parties as
necessary devices for shaping and presenting options for popular choice. In the
following selection the late Richard Hofstadter treats this very important
political transformation

I

The modern idea of the political party, and with it a fully
matured conception of the function of legitimate opposition,
flowered first among the second generation of American political
leaders—that is, among men who were in the main still children
when the Federalist and Republican parties were founded. Where
the Federalists and Republicans, still enchanted with eighteenth-
century visions of political harmony, had schemed to devour,
absorb, or annihilate each other, many Republicans raised on the
one-party politics of the misnamed Era of Good Feelings, began to
see clearly and consistently what such predecessors as Madison
and Jefferson had seen only dimly and fitfully—the merits of the
party organization as a positive principle, and of two-party
competition as an asset to the public interest. The men of the
second generation built firmly upon the foundations of early
Jeffersonian experience with the organization of the party, but in
both theory and practice they went well beyond their predecessors.

Here I propose to look at the history of the Republican party in
New York State, to take the men of the so-called Albany Regency
as archetypes of the new advocates of party, and to focus upon
their leader Martin Van Buren, an intelligent and seasoned
exponent of the emerging partisan creed, and the first representative of the new generation and mentality to become President. In
settling upon New York as the archetype of these changes, I do not
suggest that they were taking place only there: quite the contrary,
what makes New York significant is that it was only the first
political center—first surely in point of importance and artic-
ulateness, and perhaps also in point of time—to manifest clearly
the new valuation of party. Along with Pennsylvania, New York

had long been a leading state in developing a politics that approximated a consistent two-party rivalry, and it was natural that it should take the lead in the party revival.

The new apologia for partisan politics was in some considerable measure the work of a generation and a type. Its leading exponents were men who, in the main, were born during the years of the early party battles or who, like Van Buren himself, came of age during Jefferson's presidency and took the first Republican President as their model of a political hero. As children they were raised on hero tales of the Revolution. As youths they saw an established two-party competition in action, then in decline. As young men making their own places in the civic order under different conditions, they could look back upon the years from 1790 to about 1812 with a new perspective and with at least a trace of detachment; and, for all their firm Republican loyalties, they could see merit in some items of the Hamiltonian program which their own party had in fact begun to appropriate. They were considerably more interested than their predecessors in organization, considerably less fixed in their view of issues, considerably less ideological. They were less thoroughly imbued with eighteenth-century anti-party doctrines, and hence more capable of finding clues to a novel political outlook in the cumulative experience of a quarter century of political life under the Constitution.

These men provided a new type of political leader-new not in the sense that men of their kind had not long been present in American political life but rather that such men were now for the first time moving toward a place at the center of the stage. Late eighteenth-century political life in the American states had been dominated by interlocking elites and led by men of wealth and aristocratic background. Political power fell to men of status because their fellows deferred to them as the "natural" leaders of the political order. This was particularly true of continental and inter-colonial (later inter-state) affairs. But during the Revolution, the ferment of the times and the upsurge of republican faith, brought to the fore a kind of middle-or lower middle-class citizen, previously overshadowed in the establishment politics of the colonial era, who began to assume a much more forceful role in government, quite evident in the composition of the assemblies, in the new post-Revolutionary states. To a degree, the adoption of the Constitution and the domination of the early Republic by Federalist leaders marked a setback for men of this sort in national politics. But it was not more than temporary; they came surging back with the developing Republican party, and became increasingly visible not only in the state legislatures but also in Congress, especially as Jeffersonian democracy waxed strong in the Northern states after 1800. Van Buren and the Regency leaders, though hardly the first generation of men of this type, went further than their predecessors. . . .

Perhaps something of Van Buren's style came from his father, whom he remembered as "an unassuming amiable man who was never known to have an enemy," but for those who want to understand his breed of politician it is of more sociological importance that he was one of those professionals who take a friendly adversary relationship in stride as part of their daily business. This conception he carried over almost compulsively into politics. *As one reads his remarkable Autobiography,* one sees that to Van Buren one could make enemies in politics as well as friends; but the enmities (to be avoided where possible) as well as the friendships were both truly personal and not necessarily linked to political alignments. Van Buren spoke countless times of his "personal and political friends"—a repeated specification which shows that he labored under no illusion that the two were necessarily to be considered identical. But, above all, political foes might still be personal friends of a sort. Party loyalty was a sacred principle, but so sacred that it was also impersonal. Repeatedly Van Buren would assure an opponent that he held him in high esteem, and he associated on amiable terms with many Federalists. By the same token, when one suffered defeat, one expected to lose a number of perquisites and spoils to one's opponents as a part of the game—and no hard feelings.

Looking back on this aspect of his career with great pride Van Buren wrote: "My political opponents, at every stage of my public life, have with great unanimity, and with no more than justice, conceded to me a rare exemption from that personal ill will which party differences are apt to engender, nor is my breast now the abiding place of those morbid feelings and adhesive prejudices so often cherished by public men who have been thwarted in their career." . . .

It became the fixed purpose of the Republicans both to defeat Clinton in the arena of practical politics and to devise an intellectual and institutional answer to his old-fashioned moralizing view of party spirit. The ethos of the party system, which was so clearly articulated by Van Buren and the other spokesmen of

the Albany Regency group between 1817 and 1824 may be taken
as an effort to systematize the imperatives of their developing
organization and to devise an answer to Clinton's posture of the
independent old-style statesman and his standard eighteenth-
century ideas on party.

During his battle with Clinton and his first years in Washington
in the early 1820's, Van Buren appears to have arrived at a
coherent view of party politics. Formulated only in a fragmentary
way in this busy period, these views have to be pieced together out
of occasional expressions. But after 1848, with his retirement from
active politics, he began writing his *Autobiography* in the course of
which he became so concerned with vindicating his idea of party
that he also produced a long treatise on the history of American
parties, finally published posthumously in 1867. Although written
afterwards, these documents are, I believe, authentic sources on
the philosophy of party that he formulated during his active years.
If his occasional utterances in the thick of battle are supplemented
by these later elaborations, one can distinguish a reasonably full
and cogent conception of party, adequate to the purposes of a
working politician.

Van Buren did not deny that party spirit can be abused, but he
considered parties not only inevitable but fundamentally a good
thing for the public interest, when properly harnessed. "The
substitution of motives of selfish advantage," he wrote in his
Autobiography, "for those of fairness and right is the characteristic of
soulless corporations of all kinds, and political parties are very
liable to become similarly demoralized." The answer to this lay in
the high character and mutual confidence of those who conducted
party affairs. The indiscriminate condemnation of parties was
utterly pointless. Van Buren spoke of his "repugnance to a species
of cant against Parties in which too many are apt to indulge when
their own side is out of power and to forget when they come in."
"I have not, I think, been considered even by opponents as
particularly rancorous in my party prejudices, and might not
perhaps have anything to apprehend from a comparison in this
respect with my contemporaries. But knowing, as all men of sense
know, that political parties are inseparable from free governments,
and that in many and material respects they are highly useful to
the country, I could never bring myself for party purposes to
deprecate their existence. Doubtless excesses frequently attend
them and produce many evils, but not so many as are prevented
by the maintenance of their organization and vigilance. The

disposition to abuse power, so deeply planted in the human heart, can by no other means be more effectually checked; and it has always therefore struck me as more honorable and manly and more in harmony with the character of our People and of our Institutions to deal with the subject of Political Parties in a sincerer and wiser spirit—to recognize their necessity, to give them the credit they deserve, and to devote ourselves to improve and to elevate the principles and objects of our own and to support it ingenuously and faithfully."

Sound and useful party contests, of course, should be based on general principles and not on personal factionalism. Party life itself would serve as a kind of moral discipline, putting a high premium upon loyalty, fidelity, patriotism, and self-restraint. Moreover, controversies were most conducive to the general interest if they were waged between *two* parties, in what could even then already be called the national tradition. Even though the Federalists by 1814 were branded guilty of disloyalty, a retrospective view of American history showed that most of such losing causes had something to offer to the general fund of public policy and public belief.

As one recognized the legitimacy of party, so one accepted the agencies necessary to its existence—the patronage, for example, as a legitimate instrument of party cohesion and reward, and the caucus, as a necessary instrument of party decision. It was important that party members subordinate personal fancies and ambitions to the dictates of the caucus. Personal relations—both in the interest of human civility and in the public interest—should not be soured or spoiled by party antagonisms. In the ethos of the professional politician, the party became a means not merely of institutionalizing strife within manageable limits but also of cementing civic loyalty and creating a decent and livable atmosphere. Similarly, parties, if they were national and not sectional, could become valuable instruments of intersectional cohesion. Finally, Van Buren believed in the value of opposition itself as a cohesive force. It was partly on this count that he favored keeping all Federalists out of the Republican party rather than trying to incorporate them. Restore the Republican party on its clear principles, he urged, and let the Federalists carry on with theirs. Naturally, he was sure that in such a competition, the Republicans, as the more popular party, would dominate most of the time. He plainly preferred such a prospect to what he had seen in New York, where a split within the Republican ranks had given the Federalists a chance to gain leverage out of proportion to their numbers by throwing their support to one faction or another. But here, for all his desire to be a sound Republican in the Jeffersonian tradition, Van Buren was a heretic on one vital count: he accepted, he even welcomed, the idea of a permanent opposition. And this in turn marked the longest single stride toward the idea of a party system.

14 FROM   *Richard P. McCormick*
         New Perspectives on Jacksonian Politics

The popular concepts of Jacksonian democracy picture a great outpouring of newly enfranchised voters rallying with loud huzzahs around their chosen leader. Such an image calls to mind the oft-reproduced paintings, Stump Speaking *and* The County Election, *by George Caleb Bingham with their romantic idealization of shirt-sleeved, if slightly besotted, democracy.*

Recent scholarship, however, sharply challenges this traditional view, indicating that there was nothing like a great democratic upsurge in the national elections of the Jacksonian era. The work of Richard P. McCormick, a professor of history at Rutgers University, led the way in reevaluating voter participation. As McCormick writes: "The remarkable feature of the vote in the Jacksonian elections is not its immensity but rather its smallness." In 1828 a little more than 56 percent of adult white males voted; in 1832, at the height of the Bank War, this percentage had declined to slightly less than 55 percent. The only national election of the period to attract a sizable portion of the eligible electorate (about 78 percent) was the Log Cabin campaign of 1840 in which every conceivable electioneering device was used to bring out the vote.

SOURCE. Richard P. McCormick, "New Perspectives on Jacksonian Politics," *American Historical Review,* LXV (January 1960), pp. 288-301.

The historical phenomenon that we have come to call Jacksonian democracy has long engaged the attention of Anerican political historians, and never more insistently than in the past decade. From the time of Parton and Bancroft to the present day scholars have recognized that a profoundly significant change took place in the climate of politics simultaneously with the appearance of Andrew Jackson on the presidential scene. They have sensed that a full understanding of the nature of that change might enable them to dissolve some of the mysteries that envelop the operation of the American democratic process. With such a challenging goal before them, they have pursued their investigations with uncommon intensity and with a keen awareness of the contemporary relevance of their findings.

A cursory view of the vast body of historical writing on this subject suggests that scholars in the field have been largely preoccupied with attempts to define the content of Jacksonian democracy and identify the influences that shaped it. What did Jacksonian democracy represent, and what groups, classes, or sections gave it its distinctive character? The answers that have been given to these central questions have been—to put it succinctly—bewildering in their variety. The discriminating student, seeking the essential core of Jacksonianism, may make a choice among urban workingmen, southern planters, venturous conservatives, farm-bred *nouveaux riches,* western frontiersmen, frustrated entrepreneurs, or yeoman farmers. Various as are these interpretations of the motivating elements that constituted the true Jacksonians, the characterizations of the programmatic features of Jacksonian democracy are correspondingly diverse. Probably the reasonable observer will content himself with the conclusion that many influences were at work and that latitudinarianism prevailed among the Jacksonian faithful.

In contrast with the controversy that persists over these aspects of Jacksonian democracy, there has been little dissent from that judgment the "the 1830's saw the triumph in American politics of that democracy which has remained pre-eminently the distinguishing feature of our society." The consensus would seem to be that with the emergence of Jackson, the political pulse of the nation quickened. The electorate, long dormant or excluded from the polls by suffrage barriers, now became fired with unprecedented political excitement. The result was a bursting forth of democratic energies, evidenced by a marked upward surge in voting. Beard in his colorful fashion gave expression to the common viewpoint when he asserted that "the roaring flood of the new democracy was . . .[by 1824] foaming perilously near the crest . . . ." Schlesinger, with his allusion to the "immense popular vote" received by Jackson in 1824, creates a similar image. The Old Hero's victory in 1828 has been hailed as the consequence of a "mighty democratic uprising."

That a "new democracy, ignorant, impulsive, irrational" entered the arena of politics in the Jacksone era has become on of the few unchallenged "facts" in an otherwise controversial field. Differences of opinion occur only when attempts are made to account for the remarkable increase in the size of the active electorate. The commonest explanations have emphasized the assertion by the common man of his newly won political privileges, the democratic influences that arose out of the western frontier, or the magnetic attractiveness of Jackson as a candidate capable of appealing with singular effectiveness to the backwoods hunter, the plain farmer, the urban workingman, and the southern planter.

Probably because the image of a "mighty democratic uprising" has been so universally agreed upon, there has been virtually no effort made to describe precisely the dimensions of the "uprising." Inquiry into this aspect of Jacksonian democracy has been discouraged by a common misconception regarding voter behavior before 1824. As the authors of one of our most recent and best textbooks put it: "In the years from the beginning of the government to 1824, a period for which we have no reliable election statistics, only small numbers of citizens seemed to have bothered to go to the polls." Actually, abundant data on pre-1824 elections is available, and it indicates a far higher rate of voting than has been realized. Only by taking this data into consideration can voting behavior after 1824 be placed in proper perspective.

The question of whether there was indeed a "mighty democratic uprising" during the Jackson era is certainly crucial in any analysis of the political character of Jacksonian democracy. More broadly, however, we need to know the degree to which potential voters participated in elections before, during, and after the period of Jackson's presidency as well as the conditions that apparently influenced the rate of voting. Only when such factors have been analyzed can we arrive at firm conclusions with respect to the dimensions of the political changes that we associate with Jacksonian democracy. Obviously in studying voter participation we are dealing with but one aspect of a large problem, and the limitations imposed by such a restrictive focus should be apparent.

In measuring the magnitude of the vote in the Jackson elections it is hardly significant to use the total popular vote cast throughout the nation. A comparison of the total vote cast in 1812, for example, when in eight of the seventeen states electors were chosen by the legislature, with the vote in 1832, when every state except South Carolina chose its electors by popular vote, has limited meaning. Neither is it revealing to compare the total vote in 1824 with that in 1832 without taking into consideration the population increase during the interval. The shift from the legislative choice of electors to their election by popular vote, together with the steady population growth, obviously swelled the presidential vote. But the problem to be investigated is whether the Jackson elections brought voters to the polls in such enlarged or unprecedented proportions as to indicate that a "new democracy" had burst upon the political scene.

The most practicable method for measuring the degree to which voters participated in elections over a period of time is to relate the number of votes cast to the number of potential voters. Although there is no way of calculating precisely how many eligible voters there were in any state at a given teme, the evidence at hand demonstrates that with the exception of Rhode Island, Virginia, and Louisiana the potential electorate after 1824 was roughly equivalent to the adult white male population.[1] A meaningful way of expressing the rate of voter participation, then, is to state it in terms of the percentage of the adult white males actually voting. This index can be employed to measure the variations that occurred in voter participation over a period of time and in both national and state elections. Consequently a basis is provided for comparing the rate of voting in the Jackson elections with other presidential elections before and after his regime as well as with state elections.

[1] The only states in which property qualifications were a factor in restricting voting in presidential elections after 1824 were Virginia and Rhode Island. New York did not completely abolish property qualifications until 1826, but the reform of 1821 had resulted in virtually free suffrage. In Louisiana, where voters were required to be taxpayers, the nature of the system of taxation operated to confine the suffrage to perhaps half of the adult white males. See Joseph G. Tregle, "Louisiana in the Age of Jackson: A Study in Ego Politics," doctoral dissertation, University of Pennsylvania, 1954, 105-108. To be perfectly accurate, estimates of the size of the potential electorate would have to take into account such factors as citizenship and residence requirements and, in certain states, the eligibility of Negro voters.

Using this approach it is possible, first of all, to ascertain whether or not voter participation rose markedly in the three presidential elections in which Jackson was a candidate. Did voter participation in these elections so far exceed the peak participation in the pre-1824 elections as to suggest that a mighty democratic uprising was taking place? The accompanying data (Table 1) provides an answer to this basic question.

In the 1824 election not a single one of the eighteen states in which the electors were chosen by popular vote attained the

TABLE I
Percentages of Adult White Males Voting in Elections

State	Highest Known % AWM Voting before 1824 Year	% AWM	Presidential Elections 1824	1828	1832	1836	1840	1844
Maine	1812g	62.0	18.9	42.7	66.2*	37.4	82.2	67.5
New Hampshire	1814g	80.8	16.8	76.5	74.2	38.2	86.4*	65.6
Vermont	1812g	79.9	–	55.8	50.0	52.5	74.0	65.7
Massachusetts	1812g	67.4	29.1	25.7	39.3	45.1	66.4	59.3
Rhode Island	1812g	49.4	12.4	18.0	22.4	24.1	33.2	39.8
Connecticut	1819l	54.4	14.9	27.1	45.9	52.3	75.7*	76.1
New York	1810g	41.5	–	70.4*	72.1	60.2	77.7	73.6
New Jersey	1808p	71.8	31.1	70.9	69.0	69.3	80.4*	81.6
Pennsylvania	1808g	71.5	19.6	56.6	52.7	53.1	77.4*	75.5
Delaware	1804g	81.9	–	–	67.0	69.4	82.8*	85.0
Maryland	1820l	69.0	53.7	76.2*	55.6	67.5	84.6	80.3
Virginia	1800p	25.9	11.5	27.6*	30.8	35.1	54.6	54.5
North Carolina	1823c	70.0#	42.2	56.8	31.7	52.0	83.1*	79.1
Georgia	1812c	62.3	–	35.9	33.0	64.9*	88.9	94.0
Kentucky	1820g	74.4	25.3	70.7	73.9	61.1	74.3	80.3*
Tennessee	1817g	80.0	26.8	49.8	28.8	55.2	89.6*	89.6
Louisiana	1812g	34.2	–	36.3*	24.4	19.2	39.4	44.7
Alabama	1819g	96.7	52.1	53.6	33.3	65.0	89.8	82.7
Mississippi	1823g	79.8	41.6	56.6	32.8	62.8	88.2*	89.7
Ohio	1822g	46.5	34.8	75.8*	73.8	75.5	84.5	83.6
Indiana	1822g	52.4	37.5	68.3*	61.8	70.1	86.0	84.9
Illinois	1822g	55.8	24.2	51.9	45.6	43.7	85.9*	76.3
Missouri	1820g	71.9	20.1	54.3	40.8	35.6	74.0*	74.7
Arkansas	–	–	–	–	–	35.0	86.4	68.8
Michigan	–	–	–	–	–	35.7	84.9	79.3
National average			26.5	56.3	54.9	55.2	78.0	74.9

* Exceeded pre-1824 high   # Estimate based on incomplete returns
g Gubernational election   c Congressional election
p Presidential election   l Election of legislature

percentage of voter participation that had been reached before 1824. Prior to that critical election, fifteen of those eighteen states had recorded votes in excess of 50 per cent of their adult white male population, but in 1824 only two states—Maryland and Alabama—exceeded this modest mark. The average rate of voter participation in the election was 26.5 per cent. This hardly fits the image of the "roaring flood of the new democracy . . . foaming perilously near the crest . . . ."

There would seem to be persuasive evidence that in 1828 the common man flocked to the polls in unprecedented numbers, for the proportion of adult white males voting soared to 56.3 per cent, more than double the 1824 figure. But this outpouring shrinks in magnitude when we observe that in only six of the twenty-two states involved were new highs in voter participation established. In three of these—Maryland, Virginia, and Louisiana—the recorded gain was inconsiderable, and in a fourth—New York—the bulk of the increase might be attributed to changes that had been made in suffrage qualifications as recently as 1821 and 1826. Six states went over the 70 per cent mark, whereas ten had bettered that performance before 1824. Instead of a "mighty democratic uprising" there was in 1828 a voter turnout that approached—but in only a few instances matched or exceeded—the maximum levels that had been attained before the Jackson era.

The advance that was registered in 1828 did not carry forward to 1832. Despite the fact that Jackson was probably at the peak of his personal popularity, that he was engaged in a campaign that was presumably to decide issues of great magnitude, and that in the opinion of some authorities a "well-developed two party system on a national scale" had been established, there was a slight decline in voter participation. The average for the twenty-three states participating in the presidential contest was 54.9 per cent. In fifteen states a smaller percentage of the adult white males went to the polls in 1832 than in 1828. Only five states bettered their pre-1824 highs. Again the conclusion would be that it was essentially the pre-1824 electorate—diminished in most states and augmented in a few—that voted in 1832. Thus, after three Jackson elections, sixteen states had not achieved the proportions of voter participation that they had reached before 1824. The "new democracy" had not yet made its appearance.[2]

A comparison of the Jackson elections with earlier presidential contests is of some interest. Such comparisons have little validity before 1808 because few states chose electors by popular vote, and for certain of those states the complete returns are not available. In 1816 and 1820 there was so little opposition to Monroe that the voter interest was negligible. The most relevant elections, therefore, are those of 1808 and 1812. The accompanying table (Table II) gives the percentages of adult white males voting in 1808 and 1812 in those states for which full returns could be found, together with the comparable percentages for the elections of 1824 and 1828. In 1824 only one state—Ohio—surpassed the highs established in either 1808 or 1812. Four more joined this list in 1828—Virginia, Maryland, Pennsylvania, and New Hampshire—although the margin in the last case was so small as to be inconsequential. The most significant conclusion to be drawn from this admittedly limited and unrepresentative data is that in those states where there was a vigorous two-party contest in 1808 and 1812 the vote was relatively high. Conversely, where there was little or no contest in 1824 or 1828, the vote was low.

When an examination is made of voting in other than presidential elections prior to 1824, the inaccuracy of the impression that "only small numbers of citizens" went to the polls becomes apparent. Because of the almost automatic succession of the members of the "Virginia dynasty" and the early deterioration of the national two-party system that had seemed to be developing around 1800, presidential elections did not arouse voter interest as much as did those for governor, state legislators, or even members of Congress. In such elections at the state level the "common man" was stimulated by local factors to cast his vote, and he frequently responded in higher proportions than he did to the later stimulus provided by Jackson.

[2]It may be suggested that it is invalid to compare voter participation in each state in the presidential contests of 1824, 1828, and 1832 with the highs, rather than the average participation in each state prior to 1824. The object of the comparison is to ascertain whether the Jackson elections brought voters to the polls in unprecedented numbers, as has so often been asserted. Moreover, it is hardly feasible to compare average participation in elections before and after 1824 in many states because of the changes that were made in the methods of electing governors and presidential electors or—in certain instances—because the state had only recently entered the Union. However, among those states in which average voter participation was obviously higher before 1824 than it was in the three Jackson elections were Alabama, Connecticut, Georgia, Massachusetts, Mississippi, New Hampshire (1809-1817), Pennsylvania, Rhode Island, Tennessee, and Vermont (1807-1815).

TABLE II

Percentages of Adult White Males Voting in Presidential Elections

State	1808	1812	1824	1828
Maine	Legislature	50.0	18.9	42.7
New Hampshire	62.1	75.4	16.8	76.5
Massachusetts	Legislature	51.4	29.1	25.7
Rhode Island	37.4	37.7	12.4	18.0
New Jersey	71.8	Legislature	31.1	70.9
Pennsylvania	34.7	45.5	19.6	56.6
Maryland	48.4	56.5	53.7	76.2
Virginia	17.7	17.8	11.5	27.6
Ohio	12.8	20.0	34.8	75.8

Note: No complete returns of the popular vote cast for electors in Kentucky or Tennessee in 1808 and 1812 and in North Carolina in 1808 could be located.

The average voter participation for all the states in 1828 was 56.3 per cent. Before 1824 fifteen of the twenty-two states had surpassed that percentage. Among other things, this means that the 1828 election failed to bring to the polls the proportion of the electorate that had voted on occasion in previous elections. There was, in other words, a high potential vote that was frequently realized in state elections but which did not materialize in presidential elections. The unsupported assumption that the common man was either apathetic or debarred from voting by suffrage barriers before 1824 is untenable in the light of this evidence.

In state after state (see Table I) gubernatorial elections attracted 70 per cent or more of the adult white males to the polls. Among the notable highs recorded were Delaware with 81.9 per cent in 1804, New Hampshire with 80.8 per cent in 1814, Tennessee with 80.0 per cent in 1817, Vermont with 79.9 per cent in 1812, Mississippi with 79.8 per cent in 1823, and Alabama with a highly improbable 96.7 per cent in its first gubernatorial contest in 1819. There is reason to believe that in some states, at least, the voter participation in the election of state legislators was even higher than in gubernatorial elections. Because of the virtual impossibility of securing county-by-county or district-by-district returns for such elections, this hypothesis is difficult to verify.

Down to this point the voter turnout in the Jackson elections has been compared with that in elections held prior to 1824. Now it becomes appropriate to inquire whether during the period 1824 through 1832 voters turned out in greater proportions for the three presidential contests than they did for the contemporary state elections. If, indeed, this "new democracy" bore some special relationship to Andrew Jackson or to his policies, it might be anticipated that interest in the elections in which he was the central figure would stimulate greater voter participation than gubernatorial contests, in which he was at most a remote factor.

Actually, the election returns show fairly conclusively that throughout the eight-year period the electorate continued to participate more extensively in state elections than in those involving the presidency. Between 1824 and 1832 there were fifty regular gubernatorial elections in the states that chose their electors by popular vote. In only sixteen of these fifty instances did the vote for President surpass the corresponding vote for governor. In Rhode Island, Delaware, Tennessee, Kentucky, Illinois, Mississippi, Missouri, and Georgia the vote for governor consistently exceeded that for President. Only in Connecticut was the reverse true. Viewed from this perspective, too, the remarkable feature of the vote in the Jackson elections is not its immensity but rather its smallness.

Finally, the Jackson elections may be compared with subsequent presidential elections. Once Jackson had retired to the Hermitage, and figures of less dramatic proportions took up the contest for the presidency, did voter participation rise or fall? This question can be answered by observing the percentage of adult white males who voted in each state in the presidential elections of 1836 through 1844 (Table I). Voter participation in the 1836 election remained near the level that had been established in 1828 and 1832, with 55.2 per cent of the adult white males voting. Only five states registered percentages in excess of their pre-1824 highs. But in 1840 the "new democracy" made its appearance with explosive suddenness.

In a surge to the polls that has rarely, if ever, been exceeded in any presidential election, four out of five (78.0 per cent) of the adult white males cast their votes for Harrison or Van Buren. This new electorate was greater than that of the Jackson period by more than 40 per cent. In all but five states—Vermont, Massachusetts, Rhode Island, Kentucky, and Alabama—the peaks of voter participation reached before 1824 were passed. Fourteen of the twenty-five states involved set record highs for voting that were not to be broken through-out the remainder of the ante bellum period. Now, at last, the common man—or at least the man who previously had not been sufficiently aroused to vote in presidential elections—cast his weight into the political balance. This "Tippecanoe democracy," if such a label is permissible, was of a different order of magnitude from the Jacksonian democracy. The elections in which Jackson figured brought to the polls only those men who were accustomed to voting in state or national elections, except in a very few states. The Tippecanoe canvass witnessed an extraordinary expansion of the size of the presidential electorate far beyond previous dimensions. It was in 1840, then, that the "roaring flood of the new democracy" reached its crest. And it engulfed the Jacksonians.

The flood receded only slightly in 1844, when 74.9 per cent of the estimated potential electorate went to the polls. Indeed, nine states attained their record highs for the period. In 1848 and 1852 there was a general downward trend in voter participation, followed by a modest upswing in 1856 and 1860. But the level of voter activity remained well above that of the Jackson elections. The conclusion to be drawn is that the "mighty democratic uprising" came after the period of Jackson's presidency.

Now that the quantitative dimensions of Jacksonian democracy as a political phenomenon have been delineated and brought into some appropriate perspective, certain questions still remain to be answered. Granted that the Jacksonian electorate—as revealed by the comparisons that have been set forth—was not really very large, how account for the fact that voter participation doubled between the elections of 1824 and 1828? It is true that the total vote soared from around 359,000 to 1,155,400 and that the percentage of voter participation more than doubled. Traditionally, students of the Jackson period have been impressed by this steep increase in voting and by way of explanation have identified the causal factors as the reduction of suffrage qualifications, the democratic influence of the West, or the personal magnetism of Jackson. The validity of each of these hypotheses needs to be reexamined.

In no one of the states in which electors were chosen by popular vote was any significant change made in suffrage qualifications between 1824 and 1828. Subsequently, severe restrictions were maintained in Rhode Island until 1842, when some liberalization was effected, and in Virginia down to 1850. In Louisiana, where the payment of a tax was a requirement, the character of the state tax system apparently operated to restrict the suffrage at least as late as 1845. Thus with the three exceptions noted, the elimination of suffrage barriers was hardly a factor in producing an enlarged electorate during the Jackson and post-Jackson periods. Furthermore, all but a few states had extended the privilege of voting either to all male taxpayers or to all adult male citizens by 1810. After Connecticut eliminated its property qualification in 1818, Massachusetts in 1821, and New York in 1821 and 1826, only Rhode Island, Virginia, and Louisiana were left on the list of "restrictionist" states. Neither Jackson's victory nor the increased vote in 1828 can be attributed to the presence at the polls of a newly enfranchised mass of voters.

Similarly, it does not appear that the western states led the way in voter participation. Prior to 1824, for example, Ohio, Indiana, and Illinois had never brought to the polls as much as 60 per cent of their adult white males. Most of the eastern states had surpassed that level by considerable margins. In the election of 1828 six states registered votes in excess of 70 per cent of their adult white male populations. They were in order of rank: New Hampshire, Maryland, Ohio, New Jersey, Kentucky, and New York. The six leaders in 1832 were: New Hampshire, Kentucky, Ohio, New York, New Jersey, and Delaware. It will be obvious that the West, however that region may be defined, was not leading the "mighty democratic uprising." Western influences, then, do not explain the increased vote in 1828.

There remains to be considered the factor of Jackson's personal popularity. Did Jackson, the popular hero, attract voters to the polls in unprecedented proportions? The comparisons that have already been made between the Jackson elections and other elections—state and national—before, during, and after his presidency would suggest a negative answer to the question. Granted that a majority of the voters in 1828 favored Jackson, it is not evident that his partisans stormed the polls any more enthusiastically than did the Adams men. Of the six highest states in voter participation in 1828, three favored Adams and three were for Jackson, which could be interpreted to mean that the convinced Adams supporters turned out no less zealously for their man than did the ardent Jacksonians. When Van Buren replaced Jackson in 1836, the voting average increased slightly over 1832. And, as has been demonstrated, the real manifestation of the "new democracy" came not in 1828 but in 1840.

The most satisfactory explanation for the increase in voter participation between 1824 and 1828 is a simple and obvious one.

During the long reign of the Virginia dynasty, interest in presidential elections dwindled. In 1816 and 1820 there had been no contest. The somewhat fortuitous termination of the Virginia succession in 1824 and the failure of the congressional caucus to solve the problem of leadership succession threw the choice of a President upon the electorate. But popular interest was dampened by the confusion of choice presented by the multiplicity of candidates, by the disintegration of the old national parties, by the fact that in most states one or another of the candidates was so overwhelmingly popular as to forestall any semblance of a contest, and possibly by the realization that the election would ultimately be decided by the House of Representatives. By 1828 the situation had altered. There were but two candidates in the field, each of whom had substantial sectional backing. A clear-cut contest impended, and the voters became sufficiently aroused to go to the polls in moderate numbers.

One final question remains. Why was the vote in the Jackson elections relatively low when compared with previous and contemporary state elections and with presidential votes after 1840? The answer, in brief, is that in most states either Jackson or his opponent had such a one-sided advantage that the result was a foregone conclusion. Consequently there was little incentive for the voters to go to the polls.

This factor can be evaluated in fairly specific quantitative terms. If the percentage of the total vote secured by each candidate in each state in the election of 1828 is calculated, the difference between the percentages can be used as an index of the closeness, or one-sidedness, of the contest. In Illinois, for example, Jackson received 67 per cent of the total vote and Adams, 33; the difference—thirty-four points—represents the margin between the candidates. The average difference between the candidates, taking all the states together, was thirty-six points. Expressed another way this would mean that in the average state the winning candidate received more than twice the vote of the loser. Actually, this was the case in thirteen of the twenty-two states (see Table III). Such a wide margin virtually placed these states in the "no contest" category.

A remarkably close correlation existed between the size of the voter turnout and the relative closeness of the contest. The six states previously listed as having the greatest voter participation in 1828 were among the seven states with the smallest margin of

TABLE III
Differential between Percentages of Total Vote Obtained by
Major Presidential Candidates, 1828 to 1844

State	1828	1832	1836	1840	1844
Maine	20	10	20	1	13
New Hampshire	7	13	50	11	19
Vermont	50	10	20	29	18
Massachusetts	66	30	9	16	12
Rhode Island	50	14	6	23	20
Connecticut	50	20	1	11	5
New York	2	4	9	4	1
New Jersey	4	1	1	4	1
Pennsylvania	33	16	4	1	2
Delaware	–	2	6	10	3
Maryland	2	1	7	8	5
Virginia	38	50	13	1	6
North Carolina	47	70	6	15	5
Georgia	94	100	4	12	4
Kentucky	1	9	6	29	8
Tennessee	90	90	16	11	1
Louisiana	6	38	3	19	3
Alabama	80	100	11	9	18
Mississippi	60	77	2	7	13
Ohio	3	3	4	9	2
Indiana	13	34	12	12	2
Illinois	34	37	10	2	12
Missouri	41	32	21	14	17
Arkansas	–	–	28	13	26
Michigan	–	–	9	4	6
Average differential	36	36	11	11	9

difference between the candidates. The exception was Louisiana, where restrictions on the suffrage curtailed the vote. Even in this instance, however, it is significant that voter participation in Louisiana reached a record high. In those states, then, where there was a close balance of political forces the vote was large, and conversely, where the contest was very one sided, the vote was low.

Most of the states in 1828 were so strongly partial to one or another of the candidates that they can best be characterized as one-party states. Adams encountered little opposition in New England, except in New Hampshire, and Jackson met with hardly any resistance in the South. It was chiefly in the middle states and the older West that the real battle was waged. With the removal of Adams from the scene after 1828, New England became less of a one-party section, but the South remained extremely one sided.

Consequently it is not surprising that voter participation in 1832 failed even to match that of 1828.

Here, certainly, is a factor of crucial importance in explaining the dimensions of the voter turnout in the Jackson elections. National parties were still in a rudimentary condition and were highly unbalanced from state to state. Indeed, a two-party system scarcely could be said to exist in more than half of the states until after 1832. Where opposing parties had been formed to contest the election, the vote was large, but where no parties, or only one, took the field, the vote was low. By 1840, fairly well-balanced parties had been organized in virtually every state. In only three states did the margin between Harrison and Van Buren exceed twenty points, and the average for all the states was only eleven points. The result was generally high voter participation.[3]

When Jacksonian democracy is viewed from the perspectives employed in this analysis, its political dimensions in so far as they relate to the behavior of the electorate can be described with some precision. None of the Jackson elections involved a "mighty democratic uprising" in the sense that voters were drawn to the polls in unprecedented proportions. When compared with the peak participation recorded for each state before 1824, or with contemporaneous gubernatorial elections, or most particularly with the vast outpouring of the electorate in 1840, voter participation in the Jackson elections was unimpressive. The key to the relatively low presidential vote would seem to be the extreme political imbalance that existed in most states as between the Jacksonians and their opponents. Associated with this imbalance was the immature development of national political parties. Indeed, it can be highly misleading to think in terms of national parties in connection with the Jackson elections. As balanced, organized parties subsequently made their appearance from state to state, and voters were stimulated by the prospect of a genuine contest, a

---

[3] Careful analysis of the data in Table III will suggest that there were three fairly distinct stages in the emergence of a nationally balanced two-party system. Balanced parties appeared first in the middle states between 1824 and 1828. New England remained essentially a one-party section until after Adams had passed from the scene; then competing parties appeared. In the South and the newer West, a one-party dominance continued until divisions arose over who should succeed Jackson. Sectional loyalties to favorite sons obviously exerted a determining influence on presidential politics, and consequently on party formation, in the Jackson years.

marked rise in voter participation occurred. Such conditions did not prevail generally across the nation until 1840, and then at last the "mighty democratic uprising" took place.

15 FROM   *Lee Benson*
        Jacksonian Democracy—Concept or Fiction?

From the time of Frederick Jackson Turner and Charles Beard to the publication of Arthur M. Schlesinger, Jr.'s Age of Jackson *in 1945, it was assumed that the political victory of the Jacksonians signified the successful emergence of the common man in American politics and the triumph of democracy.*

Recent scholarship, however, has challenged this traditional interpretation. Marvin Meyers (selection 8), for instance, reverses the time-honored labels. His Whigs become the liberal party of hope, while the Jacksonians become the conservative party of fear trying to recapture the Old Republic. Richard P. McCormick (selection 18) has criticized the notion of a sudden flowering of political participation and democracy in the late 1820's and 1830's.

One outgrowth of the new revisionism has been a questioning of the concept "Jacksonian Democracy." Lee Benson has been the strongest critic of this generalizing label. After a careful study of political behavior in New York State during the second quarter of the nineteenth century, Benson concludes that none of the underlying assumptions implicit in the term Jacksonian Democracy are valid. His reasons follow.

History never repeats itself, historians do. Commenting upon this phenomenon, Thomas C. Cochran estimates that "history probably suffers more than any other discipline from the tyranny of persuasive rhetoric." To illustrate his point, he observes that "A. M. Schlesinger, Jr. and Joseph Dorfman . . . may argue

SOURCE. Lee Benson, *The Concept of Jacksonian Democracy: New York as a Test Case* (copyright 1961 by Princeton University Press; Princeton Paperback, 1970), pp. 329–335. Reprinted by permission of Princeton University Press

about the interpretation of 'Jacksonian Democracy,' but they both accept the traditional concept as central to the synthesis of the period." Following his lead, I have focused upon two questions: What empirical phenomena can logically be designated by the concept Jacksonian Democracy? Does the traditional concept help us to understand the course of American history after 1815?

A. The Concept of Jacksonian Democracy

Although all concepts are logical abstractions, they refer to some empirical phenomena. By definition, they refer "either to a class of phenomena or to certain aspects or characteristics that a range of phenomena have in common . . . . [Concepts] are abstractions from reality, designating types of movements, persons, behavior, or other classes of phenomena."

Analysis of the concept of Jacksonian Democracy reveals that every version contains these elements: 1) Andrew Jackson and his successors led (really or symbolically) a particular political party; 2) the party drew its leaders from certain socioeconomic classes or groups; 3) the party received strong mass support from certain socioeconomic classes or groups; 4) the party formulated and fought for an egalitarian ideology that envisioned not only political but social and economic democracy; 5) the party implemented a program derived from or consonant with its egalitarian ideology; 6) the opposing party drew its leaders and mass support from different socioeconomic classes and social groups, and opposed egalitarian ideas and policies.

Having identified the kinds of phenomena and relationships that are designated by the concept, we can go on to ask: did those phenomena and relationships exist in reality during the "middle period" of American history? For example, did the Jackson Party advocate and implement a program of economic democracy and social reform? Or is it more accurate to say that, in general, the Jackson Party denounced and fought against such programs?

1. Changing Definitions of the Concept

To my knowledge, no one has shown that contemporaries used the term Jacksonian Democracy to designate the ideology, values, attitudes, principles, and policies of Jackson Men, the contemporary term for men who supported the Republican Party. At present, we cannot be sure who *invented* the Jacksonian Democracy concept or when historians generally began to accept it. But the concept seems to derive from the frontier thesis associated with Frederick Jackson Turner and to have won general acceptance soon after 1900. We can be sure, however, that it has meant and now means very different things to different historians, and that attempts to clarify its meaning constitute a major field of work in American historiography. If at this late date the concept remains unclarified, it seems reasonable to doubt that it is solidly based in reality.

When we examine the literature over time, we find that historians, in trying to abstract from reality a set of phenomena and relationships that could be subsumed under the Jacksonian Democracy concept, had to make assumptions that later proved untenable. In other words, when they systematically collected data that discredited earlier assumptions, they retained the concept by redefining it on the basis of still other erroneous assumptions.

No matter how the concept has been defined, it has assumed that a strong causal relationship existed between Andrew Jackson's real or symbolic role in politics and the progress of movements dedicated to egalitarian and humanitarian ideals or objectives. It has also assumed that during the period from 1825 to 1850, both on leadership and mass levels, party battles represented reasonably clear-cut ideological and political conflicts between two types of men. In different versions of the concept, the types of men are identified by different criteria, for example, "frontier democrats" and supporters of "the old established order," "liberals and conservatives," "the business community and the other sections of society," "enterprisers and capitalists." No matter how the concept is defined, as I read the source materials and analyze the data, its underlying assumptions are, at least for New York, untenable.

2. Concept versus Reality

Taking New York as a test case, this book has tried to show the existence of an unbridgeable gap between historical reality and the concept's assumptions about the leadership, mass support, ideology, and program of the Jackson Party. "Old Hero," it is true, served as the party's rallying symbol. But the other assumptions of the concept conflict with the available evidence.

The leadership of the New York Democratic Party does not appear to have been recruited from "the other sections of society" that allegedly struggled "to restrain the power of the business community"—to cite Arthur M. Schlesinger, Jr.'s, version of the concept. Neither Schlesinger's version, nor any other version that assumes there were significant differences in the class nature of party leadership, appears credible. Instead, the evidence indicates that the same socioeconomic groups provided leadership for both parties.

We have also seen that in New York the concept makes erroneous assumptions about the class nature of mass support for the major parties. In one form or another historians have tended to accept Martin Van Buren's analysis, but the evidence discredits his claims that the Jackson Party championed the "producers" against the "special interests." According to his persuasive rhetoric, the Jacksonians took the side of the producers in the conflict between "those who live by the sweat of their brow and those who live by their wits." When we penetrated the rhetorical surface and struck hard data, however, we found that farmers, mechanics, and "working classes" did not form the "main-stay of the Democratic party." Instead of low-status socioeconomic groups, the Jacksonians' strongest support came from relatively high-status socioeconomic groups in the eastern counties, and relatively low-status *ethnocultural and religious groups* in all sections of New York.

Politically hard-pressed by the People's Party, the Antimasonic Party, the Working Men's Party, and finally the Whig Party, the Van Buren faction and then the Jackson Party eventually capitulated and adopted the egalitarian ideology advocated by their opponents. But, contrary to the assumptions of the concept, the Jackson Party attacked rather than sponsored the Whig idea of the positive liberal state functioning to "equalize the condition of men" by enabling "the people to act in a joint and vigorous concert for the common good. . . [or, as the Founding Fathers phrased it] the general welfare."

Moreover, if action is the real test of doctrine, the Jackson Party in New York stood firmly by its ideology. Instead of vigorously implementing, it uncompromisingly opposed political programs that required the state to act positively to foster democratic egalitarianism, economic democracy, social and humanitarian reform. How then can we reconcile the actual ideology and program with any version of the concept?

The evidence suggests that in New York Jacksonian Democracy can designate men who shared only one general characteristic: after 1828 they voted for candidates nominated by the Rpublican Party. That party expressed a particular ideology and implemented a program consonant with it, but its ideology and program derived from the old doctrines of state rights, strong executive, freedom of conscience, and the new doctrine of negative government. But why equate those doctrines with democracy? Why make the party that advocated them either the champion or the instrument of the democratic, egalitarian, humanitarian movements that emerged during the second quarter of the nineteenth century? Both on logical and empirical grounds, it seems a more credible hypothesis that in New York those movements progressed in spite of rather than because of the "Jackson Men" and the "Jackson Party."

3. Is the Concept Useful?

In addition to asking what empirical phenomena can logically be designated by the Jacksonian Democracy concept, I have raised the question whether the concept helps us to understand the course of American history after 1815. Since the present book has focused upon a single state, I cannot pretend to have answered that question convincingly. But two conclusions do appear to be warranted: 1) The concept of Jacksonian Democracy has obscured rather than illuminated the course of *New York* history after 1815, has distracted historians from the significance of their own work, and has led them to offer interpretations that are contradicted by their own findings. 2) Since events in New York are invariably cited by historians who accept some version of the concept, systematic research may find that in other states the concept also does not conform to reality. These two conclusions receive additional support when we examine one of the most recent, and in many respects most penetrating, studies of the period.

In what may well come to be regarded as a classic study of banking in America, Bray Hammond argues that the Jacksonian "cause was a sophisticated one of enterpriser against capitalist, of banker against regulation, and of Wall Street against Chestnut." The last phrase refers to the New York City bankers who, Hammond claims, played leading roles in the campaign to defeat recharter of the Bank of the United States, operating out of Philadelphia headquarters. Writing in a characteristically ironic vein, he asserts that the "Jacksonian revolution" democratized business "under a great show of agrarian idealism" by humbly-born, rugged individualists who "made the age of Jackson a festival of *laissez faire* prelusive to the Age of Grant and the robber barons." And he streses heavily the idea that Jacksonians came up from the farm to do battle with "the established urban capitalists, mercantile and financial": "In their attack on the Bank of the United States, the Jacksonians still employed the vocabulary of their agrarian backgrounds. The phraseology of idealism was adapted to money-making, the creed of an earlier generation becoming the cant of its successor. Their terms of abuse were 'oppression,' 'tyranny,' 'monied power,' 'aristocracy,' 'wealth,' 'privilege,' 'monopoly,' their terms of praise were 'the humble,' 'the poor,' 'the simple,' 'the honest and the industrious. . . .' Neither the President, nor his advisers, nor their followers saw any discrepancy between the concept of freedom in an age of agrarian-ism and the concept of freedom in one of enterprise. . . . Not-withstanding their language, therefore, the Jacksonians' destruc-tion of the Bank of the United States was in no sense a blow at capitalism or property or the 'money power.' It was a blow at an older set of capitalists by a newer, more numerous set. It was incident to the democratization of business, the diffusion of enterprise among the mass of people, and the transfer of economic primacy from an old and conservative merchant class to a newer, more aggressive, and more numerous body of business men and speculators of all sorts."

In my opinion, Hammond's treatment of the democratization of business after 1825 represents a major contribution to American historiography and lights the way to further progress. But, as I have tried to show while tracing the movement for free banking, his own researches help to refute the assumption that business democratization in New York must primarily be attributed to farm-born Jacksonians of humble background, *or to any other kind of Jacksonians*. Attention is directed here toward showing how, in the passages quoted above, the Jacksonian Democracy concept imposes severe strains upon logical consistency.

Were not many of the Wall Street and other New York bankers who worked to destroy the Bank of the United States the very archetypes of the "established urban capitalists" against whom the alleged Jacksonian revolution was allegedly directed? Did not many of those bankers hold high rank in the Republican Party of Andrew Jackson? In New York State, did they not hold either high rank or considerable influence in Tammany Hall and the Albany Regency, which contributed so much to Jackson's election? Indeed, didn't many of those bankers owe their position as "established urban capitalists" to the "monopoly charters" granted them for long and loyal service to the Republican Party? Didn't the great majority of the Jackson Party in the New York legislature oppose the movement led and supported by the Whigs to "democratize" banking? But if those and similar questions require affirmative answers— Hammond, I believe, would agree that they do—it becomes logically impossible to attribute the democratization of business in New York State to farm-born Jacksonians revolting against established urban capitalists.

Another logical inconsistency fostered by the Jacksonian Democracy concept is illustrated by Hammond's emphasis upon the "agrarian" vocabulary Jacksonians employed to attack the Bank. Were abusive terms, such as oppression, tyranny, monied power, and aristocracy, exclusively or primarily agrarian? Had they not been used by nonagrarians, too, long before Andrew Jackson became a national political figure and long before business began to be democratized? *Didn't the men who passionately opposed "King Andrew" and his party use essentially the same terms of praise and abuse as the men who passionately supported him?* Had not the Anti-masons adapted to politics the vocabulary of sectarian abuse, referred to Van Buren's Safety-Fund "scheme" as a "monster" institution, and denounced the "moneyed aristocracy, existing in the city of Albany, which owns the Mechanics' and Farmers' bank"? Why assign Jacksonians a monopoly on terms commonly used during the Age of Egalitarianism by large numbers of men in all parties? Similarly, if most Jacksonians were farm-born, were not most anti-Jacksonians also farm-born? If some established urban capitalists opposed the party of Jackson, were not others counted among his most ardent supporters? In short, before we draw conclusions about the class composition of the Democratic and Whig parties, we must systematically analyze the opponents of the "Jackson Party," as well as its adherents.

Since Hammond accepts the traditional concept as central to the synthesis of the period, he, like other commentators beginning with Tocqueville, attributes characteristics and ideas and policies to Jacksonians that, at least in New York, are either more accurately associated with their opponents or best described as common to members of both major parties. Thus he emphasizes the importance of the New York Free Banking Act; but instead of attributing its passage to the long campaign waged by the opponents of the Jackson Party (Working Men, Antimasons, Whigs), he attributes it to the groups that actually fought against the Act, the urban Locofocos and the rural Radical Democrats. Perhaps we could find no better illustration to support the conclusion that the Jackson Democracy concept has distracted historians from the significance of their own work and has forced them to operate within an inadequate framework of ideas.

16   FROM   *Francis J. Grund*

General Jackson Understands the People of the United States

Despite the scholarly criticisms of the concept of Jacksonian Democracy, there was something about President Andrew Jackson that generated strong feelings in his contemporaries. His supporters felt a great loyalty for Old Hickory and considered him as the representative of the people; his political opponents, on the other hand, pictured the General as a hateful demagogue who was bent on an unconstitutional usurpation of congressional rights. These strong emotions were the stuff of party politics and helped assure the success of the two-party system.

In this selection, Francis J. Grund, a German who had settled permanently in America, records a conversation that he held with two Democratic Senators

SOURCE. Francis J. Grund, *Aristocracy in America* (2 vols., London, Richard Bentley, 1839), II, pp. 239-246.

about the nature of Jackson's leadership. Their analysis reveals many of the values and characteristics of the age.

. . ."General Jackson," said one of the senators, "understands the people of the United States twenty times better than his antagonists; and, if his successor have but half the same tact, the Whigs may give up the hope of governing the country for the next half century."

"You ought not to say '*tact,*'" interrupted the other senator, "for that alone will not do it; he must have the same manners as our present President. General Jackson has a peculiar way of addressing himself to the feelings of every man with whom he comes in contact. His simple, unostentatious manners carry into every heart the conviction of his honesty; while the firmness of his character inspires his friends with the hope of success. His motto always was, '*Never sacrifice a friend to an enemy;*' or, '*Make yourself strong with your friends, and you need not fear your foes.* 'These things, however, must be *born* with a man; they must be spontaneous, and felt as such by the people, or they lose the best part of their effect. All the tact in the world will not answer the same purpose; for, in exactly the same proportion as we perceive a man is prudent, we become cautious ourselves—and then farewell to popularity!

"When the people give their suffrages to a man, they never do so on a rigid examination of his political principles: for this task the labouring classes of any country neither have the time nor the disposition, and it is wholly needless to attempt to persuade them to a different course by a long and tedious argument. The large masses act in politics pretty much as they do in religion. Every doctrine is with them, more or less, a matter of *faith*; received, principally, on account of their trust in the apostle. If the latter fail to captivate their hearts, no reasoning in the world is capable of filling the vacancy: and the more natural and corrupt the people are, the less are they to be moved by abstract reasoning, whether the form of government be republican, monarchical, or despotic."

"Precisely so," ejaculated the member. "General Jackson is popular, just because he is General Jackson; so much so, that if a man were to say a word against him in the Western States, he would be '*knocked into eternal smash.*'"

"And this sort of popularity," continued the senator, "our Northern people consider as the mere consequence of the battle of

New Orleans. The battle, and General Jackson's military character, had undoubtedly a great deal to do with it, but they were not
of themselves sufficient to elevate him to the Presidency. In a
country in which so large a portion of the people consider the
acquiring of a fortune the only rational object of pursuit,—in
which so great and so exclusive an importance is attached to
money, that, with a few solitary exceptions, it is the only means of
arriving at personal distinction,—a character like Jackson's, so
perfectly disinterested, and so entirely devoted to what he at least
deemed the good of his country, could not but excite astonishment
and admiration among the natural, and therefore more suscep-
tible, people of the Western States. The appearance of General
Jackson was a phenomenon, and would at the present time have
been one in every country. He called himself 'the people's friend,'
and gave proofs of his sincerity and firmness in adhering to his
friends, and of his power to protect them. The people believed in
General Jackson as much as the Turks in their prophet, and would
have followed him wherever he chose to lead them. With this
species of popularity it is in vain to contend; and it betrays little
knowledge of the world, and the springs of human action, to
believe those who possess it men of ordinary capacity. . . .

. . ."It has been said of General Jackson that he is incapable of
writing a good English sentence, as if this were the standard by
which to measure the capacity of a political chief, especially in
America, where, out of a hundred senators and representatives,
scarcely one has received what in Europe would be called a
literary education. If classical learning were to constitute the scale
by which to measure the talents of our statesmen, how far would
they not rank behind the paltriest Prussian schoolmaster! General
Jackson understood the people of the United States better than,
perhaps, any President before him, and developed as much energy
in his administration as any American statesman. I do not here
speak as a partisan, nor do I wish to inquire whether all his
measures were beneficial to the people; but they were, at least, all
in unison with his political doctrines, and carried through with an
iron consequence, notwithstanding the enormous opposition that
wealth, and, in a great degree, also talent, put in the way of their
execution. And yet they call Jackson a second-rate man, because
he is not a regular *speechifyer,* or has never published a long article
in the newspapers!

"To judge of a man like General Jackson, one must not analyze
him after the manner of a chemist; one must not separate his

talents—his oratory—his style of composition—his generalship, &c.;
but take the *tout ensemble* of the man, and I venture to say there is
not such another in the United States. It is useless to draw envious
comparisons between him and Washington, Wellington, Napoleon,
Jefferson, and so forth. Great men always wear the imprints of the
times and circumstances which call their talents into action; but
history is sure to preserve the name of any man who has had the
strength and genius to stamp his own character on the people over
whose destinies he presided. General Jackson has many political
enemies, and his political doctrines are perhaps only maintained—I
will not say maintainable—by his own great personality. His
successor in office may not be able to continue to make head
against the opposition—another party may get into power, and
introduce different doctrines into the administration of the country;—but the impulse which General Jackson has given to the
democracy of America will always continue to be felt, and impel
the government in a more or less popular direction."

"You are a great friend of General Jackson," said I, "from the
animated defence you make of his character."

"I certainly am, sir," said he; "and I do not know a single man
of our party that is not warmly attached to him. Not that I
approve of all his political principles; but I like the man, and
would rather see *him* President than any other."

"You have spoken my very heart," cried the other senator. "I
like *Old Hickory*, because he is just the man for the people, and as
immovable as a rock. One always knows where to find him."

"He is just the man our party wanted," rejoined the first
senator, "in order to take the lead."

"And I like Old Ironhead," said the member, "because he is a
man after my own sort. When he once says he is your friend, he *is*
your friend; but once your enemy, then *look out for breakers.*"

"And, what is more," interrupted the senator, "his hatred is of
that pure Saxon kind which is always coupled with moral horror;
and, for that reason, irreconcileable."

"And, what is better than all," cried the member, chuckling, "he
has a good memory; he never forgets a man who has rendered him
a service, nor does he ever cease to remember an injury. The
former is sure of being rewarded, the latter will with difficulty
escape punishment. Mr. Adams, during his Presidency, was
pusillanimous enough to endeavour to reconcile his enemies by all
sorts of *douceurs*; he appointed them to office, invited them to
dinner, and distinguished them even before his friends. This

conduct naturally alienated the latter; while the former, perceiv-
ing his drift, did not think themselves bound to be grateful for his
attentions. General Jackson introduced the doctrine of reward and
punishment, and has '*got along*' with it much better than his
warmest friends anticipated. He appointed his friends to office,
and dismissed his antagonists the moment they had taken an
active part in politics. That principle, sir, is the proper one to go
upon. The hope of reward, and the fear of punishment, govern
men in politics and religion." . . .

17 FROM   *John William Ward*
                Andrew Jackson Symbol for an Age

*In a sophisticated interpretation published in the mid-1950's, John
William Ward, a professor of history and American studies at Amherst
College, tries to explain Andrew Jackson in terms of symbol and myth. As in
the preceding selection, Ward stresses the significance of Jackson's military
career, his strong will, and his intuitive wisdom. Jackson, according to Ward,
united in himself the age's three dominant concepts—Nature, Providence, and
Will. Jackson was the "symbol for an age." As Ward concludes: "To
describe the early nineteenth century as the age of Jackson misstates the
matter. The age was not his. He was the age's."*

Coda

In the preceding sections three concepts—Nature, Providence,
and Will—have been examined separately. These three ideas with
their individual connotations do not exhaust the meaning that

SOURCE. John William Ward, *Andrew Jackson Symbol for an Age,* pp. 279-283.
Copyright 1955 by John William Ward. Reprinted by permission of Oxford
University Press, Inc.

Andrew Jackson had for the imagination of his contemporaries, but they do provide the main structural elements about which his appeal took shape. They are, to use a violent metaphor, the ideational skeleton of the ideal Andrew Jackson.

Two things are to be observed about the total significance of the concepts, nature, providence, and will. First, they possess a dramatic unity; that is, all three achieve realization through one figure, Andrew Jackson, who was the age's hero in a wider sense than has commonly been recognized. Any student of American culture will quickly be able to point to other manifestations at the time of these three ideas, either singly or in conjunction with one another. This is necessarily so and is the best proof of the point I wish to make: that the symbolic Andrew Jackson is the creation of his time. Through the age's leading figure were projected the age's leading ideas. Of Andrew Jackson the people made a mirror for themselves. Now obviously Andrew Jackson, the man, offered more tractable material for the construction of a symbol that carried the meanings we have discovered in the ideal Jackson than (say) John Quincy Adams could offer. But this is less important than the obvious fact that historical actuality imposed little restriction on the creation of the symbolic role the people demanded Andrew Jackson to play. Without attempting to explore the significance of his remark, Richard Hofstadter has observed that "the making of a democratic leader is not a simple process. . .Andrew Jackson-. . .has often been set down as typical of the democratic frontiersman; but many patent facts about his life fit poorly with the stereotype." This is most obviously the case with the relation of Jackson to nature, as Hofstadter sees. It is no less true, as we have seen, with the ideas of providence and will. But this is only to prove what Carlton J.H. Hayes pointed out some years ago: "Nationalist mythology is not in every detail strictly accurate and literally true—no mythology ever is—but after all its main purpose is didactic, for example of life and instruction of manners, and didacticism need not depend slavishly upon historical or scientific fact. It claims and deserves the wider range of imagination and emotion."

The second point to be made about the ideas, nature, providence, and will, is that in addition to their dramatic unity they possess a logical unity. If only the former were true, if these three ideas had in common only a mode of presentation, one would be quite justified in disentangling them and regarding each by itself as I have done. But the process of examining each idea in isolation is artificial; it is carried out for the purpose of analysis. The concepts, nature, providence, and will, are organically interrelated; they possess a logical coherence which makes a whole and it is their total configuration that determines the symbol, Andrew Jackson.

As can be seen in most of the quotations already presented in this essay, each concept drew stength from one or both of the other two. In addition each idea usually suggests one or both of the others. For example, the idea of providence is implicit in the tutelary power of nature; the glorification of the will is permissible because providence guarantees that the world is oriented toward good; the anti-traditional aspect of nature nourishes the idea that every man has the making of his own greatness within his own determination. As we saw, the ideas of providence and will coexisted least easily; the idea that the future is your own creation is difficult to reconcile with the idea that the future has been prescribed by God. But it is not surprising that a process of the mind which can dispose of brute fact can likewise ignore the demands of internal logic. It was under the auspices of nature and providence that the cult of the self-made man prospered in America. By making God's favor depend upon each man's exertion, the people of the Age of Jackson easily reconciled personal striving with cosmic determinism, as determinists have done from Puritanism to Communism. It is perhaps possible that an age may have ideals which are mutually destructive but the ideas we have discovered in the image of Andrew Jackson are not. In their integration they make a whole stronger than any constituent part.

It is in their broad tendency, however, that the three concepts, nature, providence, and will, most fully coincide. To whatever degree each idea bolstered the others, they were all oriented in a single direction. In an age of widening horizons all three ideas sanctioned a violently activistic social philosophy. In 1815, the year in which Andrew Jackson entered upon a stage already furnished by the American imagination, *Niles' Weekly Register* observed that America was marked by the "almost *universal ambition to get forward.*" The unchecked development of the individual was the chief implication of the ideas of nature, providence, and will. It is in this respect that the figure of Andrew Jackson most completely embodies the spirit of his age.

As representative of the idea of nature, Andrew Jackson acted out the belief that training was unnecessary, that traditional learning was no more than an adornment to native sense. The theoretical result of such an attitude was the depreciation of acquired learning and the appreciation of intuitive wisdom. The practical result was a release of energy. Thought was made subordinate to action. Although it need not have done so, the theme of will tended in the same direction. The belief that man's future was his own creation could logically have led to an emphasis on the training of the individual to assure that he wrought wisely. Actually, however, the glorification of the will minimized the value of learning and training. The reason why Jackson's success was used to prove action more important than thought can be inferred from such articles as one called "Self-Cultivation" (subtitled, "Every Man is the Architect of His Own Fortunes"), in which formal education was maintained to be "but a mere drop in the sea, when compared with that which is obtained in the everyday journeyings of life." The bias of such a point of view is echoed in the statement that "in the wilds of the West [Jackson] acquired that practical form of thought which led him to look to results, and to what was to be done, rather than to matters of speculation." The argument was the same as the one that made environment subordinate to character: "all the instructions of others can do nothing for a man who does not aid himself and proceed with a fixed purpose." Thus, Jackson was described as "starting in life with a few strong natural endowments, everything besides was, with him, self made. It was he himself that improved what God had bestowed or placed near him. This eulogist had more trouble with the place of providence in the theme of the self-made man than did the person who wrote ecstatically of Jackson's first inauguration that "here, the dignity of man stood forth in bold relief,—man, free and enlightened man— owing nothing to the adventitious circumstances, of birth, or wealth, or extrinsic ornaments—but ennobled by nature—bold in conscious liberty."

The doctrine of nature which relegated the precedents of the past to the ash-heap of history released Americans to act in the present for their glorious future. No people, declared a western editor, "are so ready to make experiments respecting social relations and domestic arrangements, as those of the western country,—none. . . are so little fettered by established habits, or. . . are less disposed to consider hereditary prejudice and heirlooms which cannot be parted with." For an age eager to claim its future the past was no more than accumulated prejudice and sentimental trinkets. The future of America was in the interior because "foreign influences . . . cannot reach the heart of the continent where all that lives and moves is American."

The theme of the will more specifically relegated extrinsic circumstances to a place of minor importance. Joseph G. Baldwin extolled Jackson as "one of the Ironsides. He was built of Cromwell's stuff . . . He was incredulous of impossibilities . . . He had no thought of failure . . . there was no such word as fail. Accordingly [!] there was no such thing as failure in his history." Another asserted there was no failure because Jackson was "a Hercules of action, without learning, except that which was self-taught . . . taking [the stakes of life] by main force and commanding success by seizing the prize he sought." A society that held up for emulation this type as its ideal placed a tremendous burden on the individual. It further increased the individual's personal responsibility by implying, through the theme of nature, that the figuratively new man in America stood at the beginning of time. Both the theme of nature and the theme of will demanded tremendous exertion of the isolated man.

For the weak who might take fright at such a limitless prospect, or for the tender who might recoil from the buccaneering overtones of the theme of self-help, there was always the idea of providence. Man in America could commit himself violently to a course of action because in the final analysis he was not responsible; God was in control. Because it was believed that America had a glorious destiny, a mission, which had been ordained by divine providence, the immensity of the task facing the nation and each citizen was bathed in a glorious optimism.

The massive emotions and psychological sanctions of all three of these ideas, nature, providence, and will, converged in the image of Andrew Jackson. The result was a symbolic figure. The symbol was not the creation of Andrew Jackson from Tennessee, or of the Democratic party. The symbol was the creation of the times. To describe the early nineteenth century as the age of Jackson misstates the matter. The age was not his. He was the age's.

18 FROM *Wendell Phillips*
Public Opinion

Despite the reemergence of a boisterous two-party system in the 1830's, much activity of a political nature took place outside of party channels. The major parties were pragmatic coalitions that attempted to appeal to the broadest possible constituencies. Because of this, both Whigs and Democrats tried to ignore controversial issues. The slavery question was a good example. Politicians viewed this as a divisive, sectional issue that was to be avoided if at all possible. When they did deal with slavery, it was usually in a peripheral manner and not as a direct challenge to that institution; the dominant Democrats, in fact, were a proslavery party from Jackson's time to the Civil War. Consequently, citizens who believed that the holding of persons in bondage was a moral wrong were left with little recourse but to agitate against such injustice outside of traditional institutions.

It was during Jackson's first administration that William Lloyd Garrison and others launched the radical phase of the abolitionist movement, demanding the immediate emancipation of all slaves without compensation for their masters. One of the most brilliant and articulate of the Garrisonians was the Boston lawyer Wendell Phillips. In the following selection, Phillips defends the abolitionists, role and, in so doing, makes a strong case for the need of radical agitation outside of the established power structure in any age.

I want you to turn your eyes from institutions to men. The difficulty of the present day and with us is, we are bullied by institutions. A man gets up in the pulpit, or sits on the bench, and we allow ourselves to be bullied by the judge or the clergyman, when, if he stood side by side with us, on the brick pavement, as a simple individual, his ideas would not have disturbed our clear thoughts an hour. Now the duty of each antislavery man is simply this,—Stand on the pedestal of your own individual independence,

SOURCE. Wendell Phillips, *Speeches, Lectures, and Letters* (Boston, James Redpath, Publisher, 1863), pp. 46-48, 51-54.

summon these institutions about you, and judge them. The question is deep enough to require this judgment of you. This is what the cause asks of you, my friends; and the moment you shall be willing to do this, to rely upon yourselves, that moment the truths I have read from the lips of one whom the country regards as its greatest statesman will shine over your path, assuring you that out of this agitation, as sure as the sun shines at noonday, the future character of the American government will be formed. . . .

We live under a government of men. The Constitution is nothing in South Carolina, but the black law is everything. The law that says the colored man shall sit in the jury-box in the city of Boston is nothing. Why? Because the Mayor and Aldermen, and the Selectmen of Boston, for the last fifty years, have been such slaves of colorphobia, that they did not choose to execute this law of the Commonwealth. I might go through the statute- book, and show you the same result. Now if this be true against us, it is true for us. Remember, that the penny papers may be starved into antislavery, whenever we shall put behind them an antislavery public sentiment. Wilberforce and Clarkson had to vanquish the moneyed power of England, the West India interest, and overawe the peerage of Great Britain, before they conquered. The settled purpose of the great middle class had to wait till all this was accomplished. The moment we have the control of public opinion,—the women and the children, the school-houses, the school-books, the literature, and the newspapers,—that moment we have settled the question.

Men blame us for the bitterness of our language and the personality of our attacks. It results from our position. The great mass of the people can never be made to stay and argue a long question. They must be made to feel it, through the hides of their idols. When you have launched your spear into the rhinoceros hide of a Webster or a Benton, every Whig and Democrat feels it. . . .

There is nothing stronger than human prejudice. A crazy sentimentalism like that of Peter the Hermit hurled half of Europe upon Asia, and changed the destinies of kingdoms. We may be crazy. Would to God he would make us all crazy enough to forget for one moment the cold deductions of intellect, and let these hearts of ours beat, beat, beat, under the promptings of a common humanity! They have put wickedness into the statute-book, and its destruction is just as certain as if they had put gunpowder under the Capitol. That is my faith. That it is which turns my eye from the ten thousand newspapers, from the forty thousand pulpits, from the millions of Whigs, from the millions of Democrats, from the might of sect, from the marble government, from the iron army, from the navy riding at anchor, from all that we are accustomed to deem great and potent,—turns it back to the simplest child or woman, to the first murmured protest that is heard against bad laws. I recognize in it the great future, the first rumblings of that volcano destined to overthrow these mighty preparations, and bury in the hot lava of its full excitement all this laughing prosperity which now rests so secure on its side.

All hail, Public Opinion! To be sure, it is a dangerous thing under which to live. It rules to-day in the desire to obey all kinds of laws, and takes your life. It rules again in the love of liberty, and rescues Shadrach from Boston Court-House. It rules to-morrow in the manhood of him who loads the musket to shoot down—God be praised!—the man-hunter, Gorsuch. [Applause.] It rules in Syracuse, and the slave escapes to Canada. It is our interest to educate this people in humanity, and in deep reverence for the rights of the lowest and humblest individual that makes up our numbers. Each man here, in fact, holds his property and his life dependent on the constant presence of an agitation like this of antislavery. Eternal vigilance is the price of liberty: power is ever stealing from the many to the few. The manna of popular liberty must be gathered each day, or it is rotten. The living sap of to-day outgrows the dead rind of yesterday. The hand intrusted with power becomes, either from human depravity or *esprit de corps,* the necessary enemy of the people. Only by continual oversight can the democrat in office be prevented from hardening into a despot: only by unintermitted agitation can a people be kept sufficiently awake to principle not to let liberty be smothered in material prosperity. All clouds, it is said, have sunshine behind them, and all evils have some good result; so slavery, by the necessity of its abolition, has saved the freedom of the white race from being melted in the luxury or buried beneath the gold of its own success. Never look, therefore, for an age when the people can be quiet and safe. At such times Despotism, like a shrouding mist, steals over the mirror of Freedom. The Dutch, a thousand years ago, built against the ocean their bulwarks of willow and mud. Do they trust to that? No. Each year the patient, industrious peasant gives so much time from the cultivation of his soil and the care of his children to stop the breaks and replace the willow which insects have eaten, that he may keep the land his fathers rescued from the water, and bid defiance to the waves that roar above his head, as if demanding back the broad fields man has stolen from their realm.

Some men suppose that, in order to the people's governing themselves, it is only necessary, as Fisher Ames said, that the "Rights of Man be printed, and that every citizen have a copy." As the Epicureans, two thousand years ago, imagined God a being who arranged this marvellous machinery, set it going, and then sunk to sleep. Republics exist only on the tenure of being constantly agitated. The antislavery agitation is an important, nay, an essential part of the machinery of the state. It is not a disease nor a medicine. No; it is the normal state,—the normal state of the nation. Never, to our latest posterity, can we afford to do without prophets, like Garrison, to stir up the monotony of wealth, and reawake the people to the great ideas that are constantly fading out of their minds,—to trouble the waters, that there may be health in their flow. Every government is always growing corrupt. Every Secretary of State is, by the very necessity of his position, an apostate. [Hisses and cheers.] I mean what I say. He is an enemy to the people, of necessity, because the moment he joins the government, he gravitates against that popular agitation which is the life of a republic. A republic is nothing but a constant overflow of lava. The principles of Jefferson are not up to the principles of to- day. It was well said of Webster, that he knows well the Hancock and Adams of 1776, but he does not know the Hancocks and Adamses of to-day. The republic which sinks to sleep, trusting to constitutions and machinery, to politicians and statesmen, for the safety of its liberties, never will have any. The people are to be waked to a new effort, just as the Church has to be regenerated, in each age. The antislavery agitation is a necessity of each age, to keep ever on the alert this faithful vigilance, so constantly in danger of sleep. We must live like our Puritan fathers, who always went to church, and sat down to dinner, when the Indians were in their neighborhood, with their musket-lock on the one side and a drawn sword on the other.

If I had time or voice to-night, I might proceed to a further development of this idea, and I trust I could make it clear, which I fear I have not yet done. To my conviction, it is Gospel truth, that, instead of the antislavery agitation being an evil, or even the unwelcome cure of a disease in this government, the youngest child that lives may lay his hand on the youngest child that his gray hairs shall see, and say: "The agitation was commenced when the

Declaration of Independence was signed; it took its second tide
when the Antislavery Declaration was signed in 1833,—a
movement, not the cure, but the diet of a free people,—not the
hom opathic or the allopathic dose to which a sick land has
recourse, but the daily cold water and the simple bread, the daily
diet and absolute necessity, the manna of a people wandering in
the wilderness." There is no Canaan in politics. As health lies in
labor, and there is no royal road to it but through toil, so there is
no republican road to safety but in constant distrust. "In distrust," said Demosthenes, "are the nerves of the mind." Let us see
to it that these sentinel nerves are ever on the alert. If the Alps,
piled in cold and still sublimity, be the emblem of Despotism, the
ever-restless ocean is ours, which, girt within the eternal laws of
gravitation, is pure only because never still. [Long-continued
applause.]

19   FROM   *Edward Everett*

Education in the Western States

*Not all reformers, of course, were radicals. If reform is defined as an
attempt to change something that is believed to be corrupt or unsatisfactory,
then conservative groups like the anti-Catholic nativists or the proponents of a
totally religious Sabbath were reformers. The temperance movement and the
drive to extend education were two particular reforms that drew a great deal
of support from conservative leaders, who were fearful of the pace of change
and desirous of preserving social control. It is educational reform that is the
concern of the following selection.*

*Since the founding of the republic, numerous advocates had stressed
increased education as a necessity for the success of republicanism. But by the
1830's a new emphasis on the need for educational reform as a means for
checking unrest among the lower classes was frequently heard. Horace Mann,
the most prominent educational reformer, termed education the best method of*

SOURCE. Edward Everett, *Orations and Speeches on Various Occasions* (4 vols., 9th
edition, Boston, Little, Brown, and Company, 1878-1879), I, pp. 344-353.

turning the common man away from the "wanton destruction of the property of others." Similarly, Edward Everett in this 1833 speech appeals to wealthy Boston businessmen for funds to support a newly founded college in Ohio "to give security to your property by diffusing the means of light and truth."

I understand the object of the meeting to be, to aid the funds of a rising seminary of learning in the interior of the state of Ohio, particularly with a view to the training up of a well-educated ministry of the gospel in that part of the United States; and to consider the claims of such an object on this community.

As to the general question of the establishment and support of places of education, there are principally *two courses* which have been pursued in the practice of nations. One is, to leave them, so to say, as an after-thought,—the last thing provided for;—to let the community grow up, become populous, rich, powerful; an immense body of unenlightened peasants, artisans, traders, soldiers, subjected to a small privileged class;—and then let learning creep in with luxury; be itself esteemed a luxury, endowed out of the surplus of vast private fortunes, or endowed by the state; and instead of diffusing a wholesome general influence, of which all partake, and by which the entire character of the people is softened and elevated, forming itself but another of those circumstances of disparity and jealous contrast of condition, of which too many were in existence before; adding the aristocracy of learning, acquired at expensive seats of science, to that of rank and wealth. This is, in general, the course which has been pursued with respect to the establishment of places of education in some countries of Europe. The other method is that introduced by our forefathers, namely, to lay the foundations of the commonwealth on the corner-stone of religion and education; to make the means of enlightening the community go hand in hand with the means for protecting it against its enemies, extending its commerce, and increasing its numbers; to make the care of the mind, from the outset, a part of its public economy; the growth of knowledge, a portion of its public wealth.

This, sir, is the New England system. It is the system on which the colony of Massachusetts was led, in 1647, to order that a school should be supported in every town; and in every town containing a hundred families, the school was required to be one where youth could "be fitted for the university." On the same system, eleven years earlier, the foundations of Harvard College were laid, by an appropriation out of the scanty means of the country, and at a period of great public distress, of a sum equal to the whole amount raised during the year for all the other public charges. I do not know in what words I can so well describe this system, as in those used by our fathers themselves. Quoted as they have been, times innumerable, they will bear quoting again, and seem to me peculiarly apposite to this occasion: "After God had carried us safe to New England, and we had builded our houses, provided necessaries for our livelihood, reared convenient places for God's worship, and settled the civil government, one of the next things we longed for and looked after was to advance learning, and perpetuate it to posterity; dreading to leave an illiterate ministry to the churches, when the present ministers shall be in the dust."

Now, sir, it is proposed to assist our brethren in Ohio to lay the foundations of their commonwealth on this good old New England basis; and if ever there was a region where it was peculiarly expedient that this should be done, most assuredly the western part of America—and the state of Ohio as much as any other portion of it—is that region. It is two centuries since New England was founded, and its population by the last census fell short of two millions. Forty years ago, Ohio was a wilderness, and, by the same enumeration, its population was little less than a million. At this moment, the population of Ohio (the settlement of which was commenced in 1788, by a small party from our counties of Essex and Middlesex) is almost twice as large as that of our ancient and venerable Massachusetts. I have seen this wonderful state, and the terraqueous globe does not contain a spot more favorably situated. Linked to New Orleans on one side by its own beautiful river and the father of waters, and united to New York on the other side by the lake and the Erie Canal, she has, by a stupendous exertion of her own youthful resources, completed the vast circuit of communication between them. The face of the country is unusually favorable to settlement. There is little waste or broken land. The soil is fertile, the climate salubrious; it is settled by as truehearted and substantial a race as ever founded a republic; and there they now stand, a million of souls, gathered into a political community in a single generation!

Now, it is plain that this extraordinary rapidity of increase

requires extraordinary means to keep the moral and intellectual
growth of the people on an equality with their advancement in
numbers and prosperity. These last take care of themselves. They
require nothing but protection from foreign countries, and security
of property, under the ordinary administration of justice. But a
system of institutions for education—schools and colleges—requires
extra effort and means. The individual settler can fell the forest,
build his log-house, reap his crops, and raise up his family, in the
round of occupations pursued by himself; but he cannot, of
himself, found or support a school, far less a college; nor can he do
as much towards it as a single individual in older states, where
ampler resources and a denser population afford means, cooper-
ation, and encouragement at every turn. The very fact, therefore,
that the growth of the country in numbers has been unexampled,
instead of suggesting reasons why efforts in the cause of education
are superfluous, furnishes an increased and increasing claim on the
sympathy and good offices of all the friends of learning and
education.

What, then, are the reasonable grounds of the claim, as made on
us? I think I perceive several.

We live in a community comparatively ancient, possessed of an
abundance of accumulated capital, the result of the smiles of
Providence on the industry of the people. We profess to place a
high value on intellectual improvement, on education, on religion,
and on the institutions for its support. We habitually take credit
that we do so. To whom should the infant community, destitute of
these institutions, desirous of enjoying their benefits, and as yet
not abounding in disposable means,—to whom should they look?
Whither shall they go, but to their brethren, who are able to
appreciate the want, and competent to relieve it? Some one must
do it. These institutions, struggling into existence, must be
nurtured, or they sink. To what quarter can they address themselves, with any prospect of success, if they fail here? Where will
they find a community more likely to take an interest in the object,
to feel a livelier sympathy in the want, more liberal, more able to
give, more accustomed to give. . .?

On a theme like this, I am unwilling to appeal to any thing like
interest; nor will I appeal to an interest of a low and narrow
character; but I cannot shut my eyes on those great considerations
of an enlarged policy, which demand of us a reasonable liberality
towards the improvement of these western communities. In the
year 1800, the state of Ohio sent one member to Congress; and

Massachusetts—not then separated from Maine—sent twenty-one.
Now, Ohio sends nineteen; and Massachusetts—recently, and I am
constrained to add, in my judgment, unfairly, deprived of one of
her members—sends but twelve. Nor will it stop here. "They must
increase," and we, in comparison, "must decrease." At the next
periodical enumeration Ohio will probably be entitled to nearly
thirty representatives, and Massachusetts to little more than a
third of this number. Now, sir, I will not, on this occasion, and in
this house of prayer, unnecessarily introduce topics and illus-
trations, better befitting other resorts. I will not descant on
interests and questions, which, in the divided state of the public
councils, will be decided, one way or the other, by a small
majority of voices. I really wish to elevate my own mind, and, as
far as lies in me, the minds of those I have the honor to address, to
higher views. I would ask you, not in reference to this or that
question, but in reference to the whole complexion of the destinies
of the country, as depending on the action of the general government,—I would ask you as to that momentous future which lies
before us and our children,—By whom, by what influence, from
what quarter is our common country, with all the rich treasure of
its character, its hopes, its fortunes, to be controlled, to be
sustained, and guided in the paths of wisdom, honor, and prosperity, or sunk into the depth of degeneracy and humiliation? Sir, the
response is in every man's mind, on every man's lips. The balance
of the country's fortunes is in the west. There lie, wrapped up in
the folds of an eventful futurity, the influences which will most
powerfully affect our national weal and woe. We have, in the
order of Providence, allied ourselves to a family of sister communities, springing into existence and increasing with unexampled
rapidity. We have called them into a full partnership in the
government; the course of events has put crowns on their heads
and sceptres in their hands; and we must abide the result.

But has the power indeed departed from us—the efficient,
ultimate power? That, sir, is in a great measure as we will. The
real government, in this country, is that of opinion. Towards the
formation of the public opinion of the country, New England,
while she continues true to herself, will, as in times past, contribute vastly beyond the proportion of her numerical strength. But
besides the general ascendency which she will maintain through
the influence of public opinion, we can do two things to secure a
strong and abiding interest in the west, operating, I do not say in
our favor, but in favor of principles and measures which we think

sound and salutary. The first is, promptly to extend towards the west, on every fitting occasion which presents itself, consistently with public and private duty, either in the course of legislation or the current of affairs, those good offices which of right pertain to the relative condition of the two parts of the country; to let the west know, by experience, both in the halls of Congress and the channels of commercial and social intercourse, that the east is truly, cordially, and effectively her friend, not her rival nor enemy.

The kindly influence thus produced will prove of great power and value, and will go far to secure a return of fraternal feeling and political sympathy; but it will not, of itself, on great and trying occasions of a supposed diversity of sectional interest, always prove strong enough to maintain a harmony of councils. But we can do another thing, of vastly greater moment. We can put in motion a principle of influence, of a much higher and more generous character. We can furnish the means of building up institutions of education. We can, from our surplus, contribute towards the establishment and endowment of those seminaries, where the mind of the west shall be trained and enlightened. Yes, sir, we can do this; and it is so far optional with us, whether the power to which we have subjected ourselves shall be a power of intelligence or of ignorance; a reign of reflection and reason, or of reckless strength; a reign of darkness, or of light. This, sir, is true statesmanship; this is policy, of which Washington would not be ashamed. While the partisan of the day plumes himself upon a little worthless popularity, gained by bribing the interest of one quarter, and falling in with the prejudices of another; it is truly worthy of a patriot, by contributing towards the means of steadily, diffusively, and permanently enlightening the public mind, as far as opportunity exists, in every part of the country, to secure it in a wise and liberal course of public policy.

Let no Bostonian capitalist, then,—let no man who has a large stake in New England, and who is called upon to aid this college in the centre of Ohio,—think that he is called upon to exercise his liberality at a distance, towards those in whom he has no concern. Sir, it is his own interest he is called upon to promote. It is not their work he is called upon to do; it is his own work. It is my opinion—which, though it may sound extravagant, will, I believe, bear examination—that, if the question were propounded to us, this moment, whether it were most for the benefit of Massachusetts to give fifty thousand dollars towards founding another college in Middlesex, Hampshire, or Berkshire, or for the support of this college in Ohio, we should, if well advised, decide for the latter. We have Harvard, Amherst, Williams;—we do not want another college. In the west is a vast and growing population, possessing a great and increasing influence in the political system of which we are members. It is for our interest, strongly, vitally for our interest, that this population should be intelligent and well educated; or ignorant, and enslaved to all the prejudices which beset an ignorant people?

When, then, the right reverend bishop and the friends of the west ask you, on this occasion, to help them, they ask you, in effect, to spare a part of your surplus means for an object, in which, to say the least, you have a common interest with them. They ask you to contribute to give security to your own property, by diffusing the means of light and truth throughout the region where so much of the power to preserve or to shake it resides. They ask you to contribute to perpetuate the Union, by training up a well-educated population in the quarter which may hereafter be exposed to strong centrifugal influences. They ask you to recruit your waning strength in the national councils, by enlisting on your side their swelling numbers, reared in the discipline of sound learning and sober wisdom; so that, when your voice in the government shall become comparatively weak, instead of being drowned by a strange and unfriendly clamor, from this mighty region it may be reechoed, with increased strength and a sympathetic response, from the rising millions of the North-western States. Yes, sir, they do more. They ask you to make yourselves rich, in their respect, good will, and gratitude;—to make your name dear and venerable, in their distant shades. They ask you to give their young men cause to love you, now, in the spring-time of life, before the heart is chilled and hardened; to make their old men, who, in the morning of their days, went out from your borders, lift up their hands for a blessing on you, and say, "Ah, this is the good old-fashioned liberality of the land where we were born!" Yes, sir, we shall raise an altar in the remote wilderness. Our eyes will not behold the smoke of its incense, as it curls up to heaven. But there the altar will stand; there the pure sacrifice of the spirit will be offered up; and the worshipper who comes, in all future time, to pay his devotions before it, will turn his face to the eastward and think of the land of his benefactors.

20 FROM   *Ralph Waldo Emerson*
New England Reformers

In a lecture delivered on March 3, 1844, Ralph Waldo Emerson, the fountainhead of New England transcendentalism, described the varieties of reform then agitating the country. As Emerson indicated, virtually every American institution and habit came in for close scrutiny and, if judged corrupt or sinful, organized criticism. Emerson had much in common with the New England reformers. Like them his motivation seemed essentially religious, although he was opposed to institutionalized religion. Emerson also considered, as did most reformers, individual conscience to be a higher guide than custom, tradition, or the dictates of established institutions. However, the individualism of the transcendentalist essayist was more extreme than that of most reformers. Emerson valued the insights of individual reformers, but he opposed their collective activity. His ultimate approach to reform was narrowly conservative. Only individual regeneration, he argued, could renovate society.

Whoever has had opportunity of acquaintance with society in New England, during the last twenty-five years, with those middle and with those leading sections that may constitute any just representation of the character and aim of the community, will have been struck with the great activity of thought and experimenting. His attention must be commanded by the signs that the Church, or religious party, is falling from the church nominal, and is appearing in temperance and nonresistant societies, in movements of abolitionists and of socialists, and in very significant assemblies, called Sabbath and Bible Conventions,—composed of ultraists, of seekers, of all the soul of the soldiery of dissent, and meeting to call in question the authority of the Sabbath, of the priesthood, and of the church. In these movements, nothing was more remarkable than the discontent they begot in the movers.

SOURCE. Ralph Waldo Emerson, *Essays: Second Series* (Boston, Houghton, Mifflin and Company, 1886), pp. 239-244, 247-254.

The spirit of protest and of detachment, drove the members of these Conventions to bear testimony against the church, and immediately afterward, to declare their discontent with these Conventions, their independence of their colleagues, and their impatience of the methods whereby they were working. They defied each other, like a congress of kings, each of whom had a realm to rule, and a way of his own that made concert unprofitable. What a fertility of projects for the salvation of the world! One apostle thought all men should go to farming; and another, that no man should buy or sell; that the use of money was the cardinal evil; another, that the mischief was in our diet, that we eat and drink damnation. These made unleavened bread, and were foes to the death to fermentation. It was in vain urged by the housewife, that God made yeast, as well as dough, and loves fermentation just as dearly as he loves vegetation; that fermentation develops that saccharine element in the grain, and makes it more palatable and more digestible. No; they wish the pure wheat, and will die but it shall not ferment. Stop, dear nature, these incessant advances of thine; let us scotch these ever-rolling wheels! Others attacked the system of agriculture, the use of animal manures in farming; and the tyranny of man over brute nature; these abuses polluted his food. The ox must be taken from the plough, and the horse from the cart, the hundred acres of the farm must be spaded, and the man must walk wherever boats and locomotives will not carry him. Even the insect world was to be defended,—that had been too long neglected, and a society for the protection of ground-worms, slugs, and mosquitos was to be incorporated without delay. With these appeared the adepts of hom opathy, of hydropathy, of mesmerism, of phrenology, and their wonderful theories of the Christian miracles! Others assailed particular vocations, as that of the lawyer, that of the merchant, of the manufacturer, of the clergyman, of the scholar. Others attacked the institution of marriage, as the fountain of social evils. Others devoted themselves to the worrying of churches and meetings for public worship; and the fertile forms of antinomianism among the elder puritans, seemed to have their match in the plenty of the new harvest of reform.

With this din of opinion and debate, there was a keener scrutiny of institutions and domestic life than any we had known, there was sincere protesting against existing evils, and there were changes of employment dictated by conscience. No doubt, there was plentiful vaporing, and cases of backsliding might occur. But in each of these movements emerged a good result, a tendency to the adoption of simpler methods, and an assertion of the sufficiency of the private man. Thus it was directly in the spirit and genius of the age, what happened in one instance, when a church censured and threatened to excommunicate one of its members, on account of the somewhat hostile part to the church, which his conscience led him to take in the anti-slavery business; the threatened individual immediately excommunicated the church in a public and formal process. This has been several times repeated: it was excellent when it was done the first time, but, of course, loses all value when it is copied. Every project in the history of reform, no matter how violent and surprising, is good, when it is the dictate of a man's genius and constitution, but very dull and suspicious when adopted from another. It is right and beautiful in any man to say, "I will take this coat, or this book, or this measure of corn of yours,"—in whom we see the act to be original, and to flow from the whole spirit and faith of him; for then that taking will have a giving as free and divine: but we are very easily disposed to resist the same generosity of speech, when we miss originality and truth to character in it.

There was in all the practical activities of New England, for the last quarter of a century, a gradual withdrawal of tender consciences from the social organizations. There is observable throughout the contest between mechanical and spiritual methods, but with a steady tendency of the thoughtful and virtuous to a deeper belief and reliance on spiritual facts.

In politics, for example, it is easy to see the progress of dissent. The country is full of rebellion; the country is full of kings. Hands off! let there be no control and no interference in the administration of the affairs of this kingdom of me. Hence the growth of the doctrine and of the party of Free Trade, and the willingness to try that experiment, in the face of what appear incontestable facts. I confess, the motto of the Globe newspaper is so attractive to me, that I can seldom find much appetite to read what is below it in its columns, "The world is governed too much." So the country is frequently affording solitary examples of resistance to the government, solitary nullifiers, who throw themselves on their reserved rights; nay, who have reserved all their rights; who reply to the assessor, and to the clerk of court, that they do not know the State; and embarrass the courts of law, by non-juring, and the commander-in-chief of the militia, by non-resistance.

The same disposition to scrutiny and dissent appeared in civil, festive, neighborly, and domestic society. A restless, prying, conscientious criticism broke out in unexpected quarters. Who gave me the money with which I bought my coat? Why should professional labor and that of the countinghouse be paid so disproportionately to the labor of the porter, and woodsawyer? This whole business of Trade gives me to pause and think, as it constitutes false relations between men; inasmuch as I am prone to count myself relieved of any responsibility to behave well and nobly to that person whom I pay with money, whereas if I had not that commodity, I should be put on my good behavior in all companies, and man would be a benefactor to man, as being himself his only certificate that he had a right to those aids and services which each asked of the other. Am I not too protected a person? is there not a wide disparity between the lot of me and the lot of thee, my poor brother, my poor sister? Am I not defrauded of my best culture in the loss of those gymnastics which manual labor and the emergencies of poverty constitute? I find nothing healthful or exalting in the smooth conventions of society; I do not like the close air of salons. I begin to suspect myself to be a prisoner, though treated with all this courtesy and luxury. I pay a destructive tax in my conformity. . . .

I conceive this gradual casting off of material aids, and the indication of growing trust in the private, self-supplied powers of the individual, to be the affirmative principle of the recent philosophy: and that it is feeling its own profound truth, and is reaching forward at this very hour to the happiest conclusions. I readily concede that in this, as in every period of intellectual activity, there has been a noise of denial and protest; much was to be resisted, much was to be got rid of by those who were reared in the old, before they could begin to affirm and to construct. Many a reformer perishes in his removal of rubbish,—and that makes the offensiveness of the class. They are partial; they are not equal to the work they pretend. The lose their way; in the assault on the kingdom of darkness, they expend all their energy on some accidental evil, and lose their sanity and power of benefit. It is of little moment that one or two, or twenty errors of our social system be corrected, but of much that the man be in his senses.

The criticism and attack on institutions which we have witnessed, has made one thing plain, that society gains nothing whilst a man, not himself renovated, attempts to renovate things around him: he has become tediously good in some particular, but negligent or narrow in the rest; and hypocrisy and vanity are often the disgusting result.

It is handsomer to remain in the establishment better than the establishment, and conduct that in the best manner, than to make a sally against evil by some single improvement, without supporting it by a total regeneration. Do not be so vain of your one objection. Do you think there is only one? Alas! my good friend, there is no part of society or of life better than any other part. All our things are right and wrong together. The wave of evil washes all our institutions alike. Do you complain of our Marriage? Our marriage is no worse than our education, our diet, our trade, our social customs. Do you complain of the laws of Property? It is a pedantry to give such importance to them. Can we not play the game of life with these counters, as well as with those; in the institution of property, as well as out of it. Let into it the new and renewing principle of love, and property will be universality. No one gives the impression of superiority to the institution, which he must give who will reform it. It makes no difference what you say: you must make me feel that you are aloof from it; by your natural and supernatural advantages, do easily see to the end of it,—do see how man can do without it. Now all men are on one side. No man deserves to be heard against property. Only Love, only an Idea, is against property, as we hold it.

I cannot afford to be irritable and captious, nor to waste all my time in attacks. If I should go out of church whenever I hear a false sentiment, I could never stay there five minutes. But why come out? the street is as false as the church, and when I get to my house, or to my manners, or to my speech, I have not got away from the lie. When we see an eager assailant of one of these wrongs, a special reformer, we feel like asking him, What right have you, sir, to your one virtue? Is virtue piecemeal? This is a jewel amidst the rags of a beggar.

In another way the right will be vindicated. In the midst of abuses, in the heart of cities, in the aisles of false churches, alike in one place and in another,—wherever, namely, a just and heroic soul finds itself, there it will do what is next at hand, and by the new quality of character it shall put forth, it shall abrogate that old condition, law or school in which it stands, before the law of its own mind.

If partiality was one fault of the movement party, the other defect was their reliance on Association. Doubts such as those I have intimated, drove many good persons to agitate the questions of social reform. But the revolt against the spirit of commerce, the spirit of aristocracy, and the inveterate abuses of cities, did not appear possible to individuals; and to do battle against numbers, they armed themselves with numbers, and against concert, they relied on new concert.

Following, or advancing beyond the ideas of St. Simon, of Fourier, and of Owen, three communities have already been formed in Massachusetts on kindred plans, and many more in the country at large. They aim to give every member a share in the manual labor, to give an equal reward to labor and to talent, and to unite a liberal culture with an education to labor. The scheme offers, by the economies of associated labor and expense, to make every member rich, on the same amount of property, that, in separate families, would leave‿every member poor. These new associations are composed of men and women of superior talents and sentiments: yet it may easily be questioned, whether such a community will draw, except in its beginnings, the able and the good; whether those who have energy, will not prefer their chance of superiority and power in the world, to the humble certainties of the association; whether such a retreat does not promise to become an asylum to those who have tried and failed, rather than a field to the strong; and whether the members will not necessarily be fractions of men, because each finds that he cannot enter it, without some compromise. Friendship and association are very fine things, and a grand phalanx of the best of the human race, banded for some catholic object: yes, excellent; but remember that no society can ever be so large as one man. He in his friendship, in his natural and momentary associations, doubles or multiplies himself; but in the hour in which he mortgages himself to two or ten or twenty, he dwarfs himself below the stature of one.

But the men of less faith could not thus believe, and to such, concert appears the sole specific of strength. I have failed, and you have failed, but perhaps together we shall not fail. Our housekeeping is not satisfactory to us, but perhaps a phalanx, a community, might be. Many of us have differed in opinion, and we could find no man who could make the truth plain, but possibly a college, or an ecclesiastical council might. I have not been able either to persuade my brother or to prevail on myself, to disuse the traffic or the potation of brandy, but perhaps a pledge of total abstinence might effectually restrain us. The candidate my party votes for is not to be trusted with a dollar, but he will be honest in the Senate, for we can bring public opinion to bear on him. Thus concert was the specific in all cases. But concert is neither better nor worse, neither more nor less potent than individual force. All the men in the world cannot make a statue walk and speak, cannot make a drop of blood, or a blade of grass, any more than one man can. But let there be one man, let there be truth in two men, in ten men, then is concert for the first time possible, because the force which moves the world is a new quality, and can never be furnished by adding whatever quantities of a different kind. What is the use of the concert of the false and the disunited? There can be no concert in two, where there is no concert in one. When the *individual* is not individual, but is dual; when his thoughts look one way, and his actions another; when his faith is traversed by his habits; when his will, enlightened by reason, is warped by his sense; when with one hand he rows, and with the other backs water, what concert can be?

I do not wonder at the interest these projects inspire. The world is awaking to the idea of union, and these experiments show what it is thinking of. It is and will be magic. Men will live and communicate, and plough, and reap, and govern, as by added ethereal power, when once they are united; as in a celebrated experiment, by expiration and respiration exactly together, four persons lift a heavy man from the ground by the little finger only, and without sense of weight. But this union must be inward, and not one of covenants, and is to be reached by a reverse of the methods they use. The union is only perfect, when all the uniters are isolated. It is the union of friends who live in different streets or towns. Each man, if he attempts to join himself to others, is on all sides cramped and diminished of his proportion; and the stricter the union, the smaller and the more pitiful he is. But leave him alone, to recognize in every hour and place the secret soul, he will go up and down doing the works of a true member, and, to the astonishment of all, the work will be done with concert, though no man spoke. Government will be adamantine without any governor. The union must be ideal in actual individual-ism. . . .

BIBLIOGRAPHICAL ESSAY

For the reader who wishes to pursue further the extensive literature dealing with Jacksonian America the following bibliographical guides are helpful: Alfred A. Cave, *Jacksonian Democracy and the Historians* (Gainesville, Fla., 1964); Charles Grier Sellers, Jr., "Andrew Jackson Versus the Historians," *Mississippi Valley Historical Review*, XLIV (March 1958), 615-634; Douglas T. Miller, *The Birth of Modern America, 1820-1850* (New York, 1970), pp. 140-188; John William Ward, "The Age of the Common Man," in John Higham, ed., *The Reconstruction of American History* (New York, 1962), pp. 82-97; Edward Pessen, *Jacksonian America : Society, Personality, and Politics* (Homewood, Ill., 1969), pp. 352-393; and Glyndon G. Van Deusen, *The Jacksonian Era, 1828-1848* (New York, 1959), pp. 267-283. An interesting comparative evaluation of Arthur M. Schlesinger, Jr.'s *The Age of Jackson* and Lee Benson's *The Concept of Jacksonian Democracy* is Gene Wise's "Political 'Reality' in Recent American Scholarship: Progressives versus Symbolists," *American Quarterly,*, XIX (Summer 1967), 303-328. An appraisal of the current state of Jacksonian scholarship is Lee Benson, "Middle Period Historiography: What is to be Done?", in George Athan Billias and Gerald N. Grob, eds., *American History: Retrospect and Prospect* (New York, 1971), pp. 154-190.

General interpretive studies of the Jacksonian era include: Frederick J. Turner, *The United States, 1830-1850* (New York, 1935), an older work that treats the victory of the Jacksonians as the triumph of the democratic, frontier West; Carl Russell Fish, *The Rise of the Common Man, 1830-1850* (New York, 1927), a social history that emphasizes the egalitarian aspects of the age; Arthur M. Schlesinger, Jr., *The Age of Jackson* (Boston, 1945), a classic and very readable interpretation of Jacksonian politics in terms of class conflict; Douglas T. Miller, *The Birth of Modern America, 1820-1850* (New York, 1970), and Edward Pessen, *Jacksonian America: Society, Personality, and Politics* (Homewood, Ill., 1969), two recent studies that stress the growing inequalities of the era and the anti-democratic aspects of the Jacksonian Democrats; Marvin Meyers, *The Jacksonian Persuasion: Politics and Belief* (Stanford, 1957) and John William Ward, *Andrew Jackson:: Symbol for an Age* (New York, 1955), two sophisticated studies that attempt to analyze the era's rhetoric in terms of its psychic and mythic meanings.

Useful accounts of aspects of the period's politics are: Richard P. McCormick, *The Second American Party System* (Chapel Hill, 1966); Chilton Williamson, *American Suffrage: From Property to Democracy, 1760-1860* (Princeton, 1960); Michael Wallace, "Changing Concepts of Party in the United States: New York 1815-1828," *American Historical Review,* LXXIV (December 1968), 453-491; Robert V. Remini, *The Election of Andrew Jackson* (Philadelphia, 1963); Glyndon G. Van Deusen, The Jacksonian Era, 1828-1848 (New York, 1959), a comprehensive but pro-Whig account; Lee Benson, *The Concept of Jacksonian Democracy: New York a Test Case* (Princeton, 1961), which denies the validity of associating the Jacksonians with the advance of democracy; Joseph Dorfman, "The Jackson Wage-Earner Thesis," *American Historical Review,* LIV (January 1949), 296-306, a criticism of Schlesinger's interpretation; Richard Hofstadter, "Andrew Jackson and the Rise of Liberal Capitalism," in Hofstadter, *The American Political Tradition* (New York, 1948), pp. 45-67, an account of Andrew Jackson and his followers as expectant capitalists looking for the main chance; Leonard D. White, *The Jacksonians: A Study in Administrative History, 1829-1861* (New York, 1954); Sidney H. Aronson, *Status and Kinship in the Higher Civil Service: Standards of Selection in the Administrations of John Adams, Thomas Jefferson, and Andrew Jackson* (Cambridge, 1964), a study which finds that Jackson's appointees were an elite similar to those selected by Adams and Jefferson; James Staton Chase, "Jacksonian Democracy and the Rise of the Nominating Convention," *Mid-America,* XLV (October 1963), 229-249; Richard H. Brown, "*The Missouri Crisis, Slavery and the Politics of Jacksonianism,*" *South Atlantic Quarterly,* LXV (Winter 1966), 55-72, which emphasizes the proslavery position of the Jacksonian Democrats; Frank Otto Gatell, "Money and Party in Jacksonian America: A Quantitative Look at New York City's Men of Quality," *Political Science Quarterly,* LXXXII (June 1967), 235-252, an article which indicates that by the early 1840's New York City's men of wealth were overwhelmingly Whig.

Significant studies of the banking issues central to Jacksonian politics are: Robert V. Remini, *Andrew Jackson and the Bank War*

(New York, 1967), a pro-Jackson interpretation that asserts the political importance of the Bank War; Bray Hammond, *Banks and Politics in America from the Revolution to the Civil War* (Princeton, 1957), a classic and influential anti-Jacksonian interpretation; Thomas P. Govan, *Nicholas Biddle: Nationalist and Public Banker* (Chicago, 1959) and Jean Alexander Wilburn, *Biddle's Bank: The Crucial Years* (New York, 1967), two books favorable to Biddle; Frank Otto Gatell, "Sober Second Thoughts on Van Buren, the Albany Regency, and the Wall Street Conspiracy," *Journal of American History,* LIII (June 1966), 19-40.

Particularly worthwhile works dealing with the era's economic developments are: Stuart Bruchey, *The Roots of American Economic Growth, 1607-1861* (New York, 1968), a fine summation of recent scholarship; George R. Taylor, *The Transportation Revolution, 1815-1860* (New York, 1951), the best general economic history of the era; Paul W. Gates, *The Farmer's Age: Agriculture 1815-1860* (New York, 1962); Douglass C. North, *The Economic Growth of the United States, 1790-1860* (New York, 1966); Albert Fishlow, *American Railroads and the Transformation of the Ante-Bellum Economy* (Cambridge, 1965) and Robert William Fogel, *Railroads and American Economic Growth* (Baltimore, 1964), two somewhat contradictory quantitative studies; Peter D. McClelland, "Railroads, American Growth, and the New Economic History: A Critique," *Journal of Economic History,* XXVII (March 1968), 102-123; Joseph Dorfman, *The Economic Mind in American Civilization* (3 vols., New York, 1946-1949), good on individual economists; Paul A. David, "The Growth of Real Product in the United States before 1840," *Journal of Economic History,* XXVII (June 1967), 151-195; Peter Temin, *The Jacksonian Economy* (New York, 1969), which exonerates the Jacksonians from the charge that they brought on the panic of 1837.

Two important books that treat the intellectual and psychological impact of the era's industrialization are: Leo Marx, *The Machine in the Garden* (New York, 1964) and Marvin Fisher, *Workshops in the Wilderness: The European Response to American Industrialization, 1830-1860* (New York, 1967).

The impact of economic changes on the laboring classes is excellently covered in Norman Ware's older study, The Industrial Worker, 1840-1860 (Boston, 1924). Other aspects of laboring conditions in the Jacksonian period are discussed in the following studies: John R. Commons and associates, *History of Labour in the United States* (4 vols., New York, 1918-1935); Walter Hugins,

Jacksonian Democracy and the Working Class (Stanford, 1960); Edward Pessen, *Most Uncommon Jacksonians: The Radical Leaders of the Early Labor Movement* (Albany, 1967); William A. Sullivan, "Did Labor Support Andrew Jackson?" *Political Science Quarterly*, LXII (December 1947), 569-580. Both the declining status of labor and the rise of a new moneyed elite are the subject of Douglas T. Miller's *Jacksonian Aristocracy: Class and Democracy in New York, 1830-1860* (New York, 1967).

The anxieties of the age are well documented in Fred Somkin's *Unquiet Eagle: Memory and Desire in the Idea of American Freedom, 1815-1860* (Ithaca, 1967). Other valuable analyses of the tensions in Jacksonian America include: David Brion Davis, "Some Themes of Counter-Subversion: An Analysis of Anti-Masonic, Anti-Catholic, and Anti-Mormon Literature," *Mississippi Valley Historical Review*, XLVII (September 1960), 205-224; Clifford S. Griffin, *Their Brothers' Keepers: Moral Stewardship in the United States, 1800-1865* (New Brunswick, 1960); William R. Taylor, *Cavalier and Yankee* (New York, 1963); Barbara Welter, "The Cult of True Womanhood, 1820-1860," *American Quarterly*, XVIII (Summer 1966), 151-174; Curtis Dahl, "The American School of Catastrophe," *American Quarterly*, XI (Fall 1959), 380-390. See also the previously mentioned books by Leo Marx, Marvin Meyers, and Douglas Miller.

The most comprehensive coverage of the era's varied reform movements is found in Alice Felt Tyler's *Freedom's Ferment* (Minneapolis, 1944); the interpretive analysis in *Freedom's Ferment* is sketchy and dated, but the book is a fascinating and factual narrative history. Important studies of particular reform movements include: Louis Filler, *The Crusade Against Slavery, 1830-1860* (New York, 1960); Aileen S. Kraditor, *Means and Ends in American Abolitionism* (New York, 1969); Benjamin Quarles, *Black Abolitionists* (New York, 1969); Joseph R. Gusfield, *Symbolic Crusade: Status Politics and the American Temperance Movement* (Urbana, 1963); John A. Krout, *The Origins of Prohibition* (New York, 1925); Eleanor Flexner, *A Century of Struggle: The Woman's Rights Movement in the United States* (Cambridge, 1959); W. David Lewis, *From Newgate to Dannemora: The Rise of the Penitentiary in New York, 1796-1848* (Ithaca, 1965); Peter Brock, *Pacifism in the United States* (Princeton, 1968); Merle Curti, *The American Peace Crusade, 1815-1860* (Durham, 1929); Rush Welter, *Popular Education and Democratic Thought* (New York, 1962); Michael B. Katz, *The Irony of Early School Reform* (Cambridge, 1968). Two excellent anthologies of scholarly articles on reform are: David Brion Davis, ed., *Ante-Bellum Reform* (New York, 1967) and Martin Duberman, ed., The Antislavery Vanguard (Princeton, 1965).

The religious revivals that swept over Jacksonian America and their relation with the period's reforms are dealt with in the following: Whitney R. Cross, *The Burned-Over District: The Social and Intellectual History of Enthusiastic Religion in Western New York, 1800-1850* (Ithaca, 1950); Bernard A. Weisberger, *They Gathered at the River: The Story of the Great Revivals and their Impact Upon Religion in America* (Boston, 1958); William G. McLoughlin, Jr., *Modern Revivalism* (New York, 1959); Perry Miller, *The Life of the Mind in America : From the Revolution to the Civil War* (New York, 1965); T.L. Smith , *Revivalism and Social Reform* (New York, 1957); Charles C. Cole, *The Social Ideas of the Northern Evangelists, 1826-1860* (New York, 1954); John R. Bodo, *The Protestant Clergy and Public Issues* (Princeton, 1954); and Charles I. Foster, *An Errand of Mercy: The Evangelical United Front, 1790-1837* (Chapel Hill, 1960).

Finally, no student of Jacksonian America should omit reading some of the numerous narratives of European travelers who visited the United States during the period. These visitors brought nearly every aspect of American life under close scrutiny; the most analytical and important books by these authors read like recent works in cultural anthropology or sociology with chapters on such diverse topics as public opinion, the family, class structure, land tenure, and social values. Of the literally hundreds of works by foreign observers writter during the era, the following are especially significant: Alexis de Tocqueville, *Democracy in America* (2 vols., 1835,1840), perhaps the most important analysis of American democracy ever written and essential reading for any student of Jacksonian America; James Silk Buckingham, *America, Historical, Statistical, and Descriptive* (3 vols., London, 1841); Michael Chevalier, *Society, Manners and Politics in the United States* (Boston, 1839), a very insightful analysis; Charles Dickens, *American Notes for General Circulation* (New York, 1842), superficial but interesting reading; Francis J. Grund, *The Americans in their Moral, Social, and Political Relations* (2 vols., London, 1837), detailed and informed; Captain Basil Hall, *Travels in North America in the Years 1827 and 1828* (3 vols., Edinburgh, 1829); Thomas Hamilton, *Men and Manners in America* (2 vols., Edinburgh, 1833); Sir Charles Lyell, Travels in North America (2 vols., New York, 1845); Captain Frederick Marryat, *A Diary in America* (London, 1839); Harriet Martineau, *Society in America* (3 vols., London, 1837), a thoughtful and sympathetic study of American institutions and behavior; James Stuart, *Three Years in North America* (2 vols., Edinburgh, 1833); and Frances M. Trollope, *Domestic Manners of the Americans* (2 vols., London, 1832), a petty, carping critique of American manners and morals, but one which often hits the mark and is fun to read.